SUFFE
INNOCENT A

# SUFFERING, INNOCENT AND GUILTY

Elizabeth R. Moberly

LONDON
SPCK

First published 1978
SPCK
Holy Trinity Church
Marylebone Road
London NW1 4DU


© Elizabeth R. Moberly 1978


Filmset in 'Monophoto' Ehrhardt 11 on 12 pt by
Richard Clay (The Chaucer Press) Ltd, Bungay, Suffolk
and printed in Great Britain by
Fletcher & Son Ltd, Norwich


ISBN 0 281 03623 3

# Contents

| | |
|---|---|
| **Preface** | vii |
| **Acknowledgements** | ix |
| **List of Abbreviations** | xi |
| **Introduction** | 1 |

**1 Interdependence: Setting the Context** — 3
Man created in the image of God who is Trinity. The problem of suffering and some questions of theodicy. Theodicy and atonement.

**2 The Creator and his Creation** — 16
The kenosis of God. Aspects of redemption in the thought of St Irenaeus. The possibility of the use of natural theology. The outworking and appropriation of the atonement: a reassessment of Peter Abelard.

**3 Suffering, Innocent and Guilty** — 30
The 'equation theory' of guilty suffering. Innocent suffering and the possibility of vicarious suffering. Karma as an example of an equation theory. The differentiation of innocent and guilty suffering: the Book of Job.

**4 Dealing with Consequences** — 49
The consequences of wrongdoing. The nemesis pattern. The *lex talionis*. Primary and secondary deterrence. Reformation. Punishment as an instrument for dealing with consequences.

**5 The Symbolic Theory of Punishment** — 61
Sir Walter Moberly's theory of punishment: analysis and development. The two drives underlying theories of punishment. Overcoming the traditional dichotomy of criminological thought. The 'two orders', internal and external. Punishment, itself of the second order, is to affect its first-order referents, i.e. to forestall moral deterioration and to promote penitence.

## 6 The Reassessment of Criminological Thought  82
The development of the retributive and utilitarian schools of thought, re-evaluated in the light of the symbolic theory.

## 7 The Suffering of the Guilty, Here and Hereafter  102
Suffering and moral being. Reassessment of concepts of the afterlife: the possibility of hell—judgement—purgatory. R. C. Moberly: the difficulty of penitence, to be met by the indwelling of the Holy Spirit. The transition from natural theology to the theology of redemption.

## 8 The Theology of Penitence: A Study of the Christian Life  122
Conversion and penitence. The relation between being good and doing good in various aspects of Christian life and thought. The 'Dark Night': growth in the Christian life.

## 9 Coinherence: All Life is Vicarious  136
Forgiveness. Breakdown in interdependence and responses to this. Vicariousness as everyday, not esoteric. The 'evangelical counsels' of poverty, chastity, and obedience. The Christian solitary. Images of heaven: the communion of saints; kenosis and progression; the beatific vision.

## Postscript: Some Conclusions  149

## Special Note  153
R. C. Moberly on punishment and its relation to penitence.

## References and Notes  156
## Bibliography: General  163
## Bibliography: Thematic  166
## Index of Names  179

# Preface

This study owes much both to individuals and to my family background. The original designation of my doctoral thesis was 'Atonement and personality: the consequences of wrongdoing and the possibilities of their transformation'. This was based on the title of one of the best-known works of my great-grandfather, R. C. Moberly, one-time Regius Professor of Pastoral Theology at Oxford. Apart from a brief mention, I have not attempted to develop his work directly. I have, however, included a detailed study of the theory of punishment of my great-uncle, Sir Walter Moberly—philosopher, lay theologian, educational statesman, and eldest son of R. C. Moberly. Sir Walter's work owed much to his father's thought:

> Intellectually and spiritually, I owed everything to my father and in general was his convinced disciple. I was in wholehearted agreement with the main purport of his chapter on 'Punishment' [viz., the opening chapter of *Atonement and Personality*] and with his method of treatment. But it did not seem that the relation between the reformative and retributive elements in punishment had been quite fully worked out to its logical conclusion ... Since my father had died while I was still an undergraduate, I was never able to discuss this point with him. But my own understanding of his principles leads to a slightly different conclusion ...*

It is Sir Walter's development of this particular aspect of R. C. Moberly's thought that I have attempted to elucidate, as an indispensable part of a more wide-ranging theological study.

However, while owing much to the influence of my family tradition, I differ from it in my own starting-point. The Moberly family has been Anglican and I, by choice, am a member of the

---

* *The Ethics of Punishment*, Preface, p. 23.

Russian Orthodox Church. Thus, I have written from within the Orthodox tradition, in an attempt to express some of its insights in a work of English theology.

ELIZABETH R. MOBERLY

*Oxford 1977*

# Acknowledgements

I should like to express my gratitude to a number of individuals. In so doing, an outline of some of the coinherence underlying this study should become apparent.

First, my supervisor, the Revd Dr John Macquarrie, Lady Margaret Professor of Divinity at Oxford, for his constant encouragement and scholarly help; and my temporary supervisor, Dr John Howes, now Professor of Philosophy at Cape Town, for a term of stimulating philosophical criticism.

The examiners of my doctoral thesis, the Revd Dr Peter Baelz, Regius Professor of Moral and Pastoral Theology at Oxford, and Lady Helen Oppenheimer, for their many helpful comments.

St Hugh's College, Oxford, for offering me the Yates Senior Scholarship in Theology, with which I began my research; and my undergraduate college, Lady Margaret Hall, to which I returned on expiry of my senior scholarship.

The Houses of St Gregory and St Macrina, the Orthodox and ecumenical centre of Oxford, in which I began my thesis; Professor Nadejda Gorodetzky, in whose house it was completed; and the Fellowship of St Alban and St Sergius, for its constant stimulus to theological life and thinking.

My spiritual father, Metropolitan Anthony (Bloom), for all that he has given me in terms of prayer and everything else.

Archimandrite Kallistos Ware, for his most illuminating seminars on Byzantine theology and prayer.

His Holiness the Dalai Lama, for his help in elucidating a point in the idea of karma.

Major Ramachandra, a dear friend who is doing much to further the dialogue between Hindus and Christians.

Fr Richard Woods, O.P., and Fr Simon Tugwell, O.P., for help in the discussion of exorcism.

The Revd Dr Rowan Williams, for his suggestion that I should write on St John of the Cross.

Fr Ross Collings, O.D.C., for his discussion of Carmelite theology.

Protopresbyter Cyril Browne, of the Greek Orthodox Church in London, for his help in prayer at a point when I was finding it difficult to turn thoughts into words.

Archimandrite Sophrony, of Tolleshunt Knights monastery, for prayer.

Mother Mary Clare, S.L.G., for general works of angel-guardianship.

My spiritual mother, Sister Benedicta Ward, S.L.G., for prayer and all the support of coinherent love.

Many others, known or unknown, who have in some way helped.

I am grateful to the various individuals and libraries who have lent or given me books. I should like to name the following:

First and foremost, my great-uncle, Sir Walter Moberly, who gave me most of his theological and criminological books. Without these, this study might never have taken shape. I am also grateful to Faber & Faber Ltd for permission to quote from his book, *The Ethics of Punishment*.

The Revd Peter Bide, chaplain of Lady Margaret Hall.

Pusey House; St Stephen's House; Wycliffe Hall; and Fr Gerard Corr, O.S.M., of St Philip's Priory, Begbroke, Oxford.

Unless otherwise stated, scriptural quotations are from the New English Bible, second edition © 1970, by permission of Oxford and Cambridge University Presses.

Technical terms of Orthodox theology—from the Greek, with one stated exception—are explained as they occur in the text.

# List of Abbreviations

| | |
|---|---|
| *Adv. Haer.* | *Adversus Haereses* |
| AV | Authorized Version of the Bible |
| *JTS* | *Journal of Theological Studies* |
| NEB | New English Bible |
| NT | New Testament |
| OT | Old Testament |
| *PG* | *Patrologia Graeca* (ed. J.-P. Migne) |
| *PL* | *Patrologia Latina* (ed. J.-P. Migne) |

# Introduction

This is intended as a study of some of the presuppositions of the doctrine of the atonement. It does not in itself attempt to present yet another 'theory of the atonement', or to provide a history of such theories. Much work has already been done in this sphere, and insufficient attention seems to have been paid to the ideas underlying such theories. This study focuses on the question of suffering as the basis for a reassessment.

Suffering is a complex phenomenon. It is something broader than pain, which is a specific and measurable biological phenomenon, dependent on the nervous system. Suffering need not include pain as such, and it is not necessarily either biological or measurable. This discussion aims specifically at being an ethical study of suffering. It will examine principles rather than instances, and will attempt to discuss the fundamental issues at stake. Why, after all, do we refer to suffering as an *evil*? This is an ethical question, and it is the sphere of the ethical which I would regard as potentially most fruitful for inquiry.

The field of inquiry is limited to the consequences of wrongdoing and the possibilities of their transformation. The suffering caused independently of human agency, e.g. by flood or earthquake, lies beyond the scope of the inquiry.

In connection with wrongdoing, I propose to consider both the suffering of the innocent and the suffering of the guilty (which hereafter, for convenience will be generally referred to as innocent suffering and guilty suffering respectively). I would suggest that it has been a particular defect of studies of suffering to tend to concentrate on innocent suffering in isolation, without regard for the suffering of the guilty. This seems strange when it is borne in mind that there are two parties involved in many acts of wrongdoing, a guilty party always as well as an innocent party sometimes. Thus, if either party is to be omitted from a study of suffering stemming from wrongdoing, the omission must be justified—and I do not think that it can be.

This may equally be called a study of moral being, examined in terms of both sin and suffering, with some particular emphasis on the latter. It does not of course claim to answer all possible questions. The subject-matter is far too complex and, one might add, deeply mysterious. All our answers are likely to be partial—though this is not to preclude as much discussion as is possible of the questions raised.

# I
# Interdependence: Setting the Context

'We belong to each other'

The context of the discussion of suffering is not usually sufficiently examined. Approaches to the question frequently do not go back far enough, so as to examine their presuppositions. Man hurts man—this *happens*, but how is it *possible*? If one reflects on it, this ability to hurt and be hurt is really quite a remarkable possibility. It implies the interdependence of persons, an interdependence which may be used for good or for ill, to help or to hurt. Interdependence is the basic structure or dynamic of personal existence, as is increasingly realized and acknowledged in contemporary thought and theological discussion.

However, although the phenomenon of interdependence is receiving increasing attention, its ultimate basis is not always recognized. Here we might find the so-called 'social doctrine of the Trinity' helpful. Interdependence, we have asserted, is the basic structure of personal existence. If we take this statement seriously we cannot limit its application to human personal existence, but should look also to the life of the personal God in whom we as Christians believe. We believe in one God, who is the holy Trinity—Father, Son, and Holy Spirit, consubstantial and undivided. The reciprocal self-giving and mutual indwelling (*perichoresis*) of the Trinity is primarily a statement—so far as it is granted us to make statements—about God. But we are also told[1] that man was created in the image of God, God whom we know to be Trinity. Hence we see that the pattern of human life is to be one of reciprocity, self-emptying, and mutuality—the kenotic life we were created for and are called to, in the image of the trinitarian God. This, in theological terms, may be taken as the fundamental, ontological solidarity of human society.

Interdependence may be variously described. In the tradition of the Orthodox Church, it is known as *sobórnost*, a Russian term which tends to be translated as 'catholicity' or 'togetherness', with connotations of 'community' or 'solidarity'. Of the Fathers of the Church, it is in the Cappadocians that we find articulated the idea of man-in-society as reflecting the life of God. Though if we cared to look back further, to St Paul, we would in any case read that '... just as in a single human body there are many limbs and organs, all with different functions, so all of us, united with Christ, form one body, serving individually as limbs and organs to one another'.[2] Man created in the image of the trinitarian God, and re-created as such in Christ, is man in his proper solidarity, as spoken of by the social doctrine of the Trinity. Any other solidarity tends to be partial, the solidarity of 'Us against Them', and not the truest solidarity, of *all* together. In the life of God this is *perichoresis*. In the life of man this is interdependence, some of the implications of which have been strikingly illustrated by the twentieth-century writer, Charles Williams, who uses the images of 'coinherence' and 'the City' to describe the working of man's interdependence; and shows too how the abuse of interdependence is *in*coherence, in contrast to coinherence—the Infamy instead of the City. Another twentieth-century thinker, Teilhard de Chardin, also sheds light on man's interdependence. He speaks of love as the totalizing principle of human energy, which totalizes without depersonalizing. Union in the personal differentiates.[3] This is but what we should expect if we take seriously the thought that man is created in the image of the trinitarian God, where trinitarian distinctions and relations do not detract from, but enhance, the genuine unity and oneness. A God who was—*per impossibile*—one in a unitarian sense, would be neither personal nor the creator of persons. God *is* one, in the sense that there is none beside him—this is the meaning of monotheism—but he is not merely one in his 'internal constitution', so to speak. In the words of one of the Fathers, God is one 'not in number, but in nature'.[4] Monotheism is not to be confused with monarchianism or unitarianism.

God is one, but not simple. For ancient philosophers simplicity was the highest category and, in making use of the contemporary philosophical framework, theologians too spoke of God in such terms as 'simple and uncompounded'.[5] The phrase not only guarded (properly) against crude concepts of multiplicity, but would also, if pressed literally, do less than justice to the trinitarian relatedness which is the distinctive insight of the Christian understanding of monotheism. The unity of God must be safeguarded, but unity does not—except in strictly arithmetical terms—necessitate simplicity. It is opposed to multiplicity, but not to complexity. Biological evidence suggests that life requires complexity, and that the higher the forms of life the greater their complexity. In the understanding of Teilhard de Chardin complexity has replaced simplicity as the highest category. All this is consonant with the understanding of human society as called to be coinherent (united in complexity), as God One-in-Trinity is coinherent.

The basic structure is interdependence, and human freedom is to be set against this background. Man is free to help or to hurt. It is not being assumed that 'to do good' may be translated exclusively in terms of 'to help' or that 'to do ill' is no more than 'to hurt', but it is being insisted that the discussion of personal goodness and badness is to be firmly located within the context of interdependence. Otherwise there is a tendency to think in atomistic terms, to see good and bad as static or abstract and to underestimate their personal implications, thus distorting the perspective for the discussion of sin and suffering. Yet if reciprocity is fundamental, this reflects on the nature of good and bad and implies that they must be interpreted dynamically and relationally, as aspects of the functioning or malfunctioning of interdependence. Goodness implies the kenosis involved in mutual self-giving. Badness implies the absence of this. Thus, the options of personal life are not so much good-relatedness as opposed to bad-relatedness, if one understands by this two entirely unconnected alternatives. There is one option only, of relatedness or interdependence, which may be taken up in either of two ways, good or bad, proper use or abuse. Although the basic structure can be abused, it cannot be denied. There is no alternative to interdependence for personal life—nor is any alternative conceivable, if indeed this is something true of the godhead, and not just a contingent possibility actualized in the human race.

Partly as an aside, we should add that interdependence is something larger than the 'I-Thou' relationship, though this is included within it. The limitation of the 'I-Thou' relationship is that it refers to two persons only. Yet several things suggest that one must take into account the reality of the 'third person'. Human existence obviously suggests it. A given 'I-Thou' relationship does not include all human persons, but it may not thereby discount or devalue them. In marriage, the union of the married couple will often find a particular fulfilment in the presence of a third—the child. In grammar one takes into account the first, second, and third persons, since it is realized that two categories alone are incapable of expressing every type of personal existence, though more than three are not needed or even conceivable. And there is the Trinity. God is not one in a unitarian sense, though he is *One*-in-Three. Nor, interestingly, is he two persons, namely, Father and Son. There is also the third person, the Holy Spirit, and in this threeness of persons there is the fullness of godhead. Why this should be one does not know, but all these points taken together suggest that it is important to bear in mind the category of the third person, and that to think in terms of two—however profoundly—is inadequate to do justice to the fullness of personal existence.

One lives *from* others as well as *for* others, but discussions of inter-relatedness tend to focus too much on the latter aspect and neglect the former. Yet the fact of our *derivation*, our living *from* others, is also fundamental. It is presupposed in all persons: the influence of others, in particular our families or family-substitutes, has shaped us to be what we are. Breakdown in derivation, in this basic givenness of relationship, leads to disturbance of personality. For it is through being loved that we learn to love in turn—this is the true order of things. We have to be given to, since we are not self-sufficient. But we are not given to, in order to possess, as this would be to check and stifle the dynamic of interdependence. We must ourselves give and, if we do not, we lose even what we have. 'Whosoever will save his life shall lose it: but whosoever will lose his life for my sake, the same shall save it.'[6] 'Being related to' must lead on to 'relating to', in which it finds its fulfilment.

It is clear that the framework of interdependence suggests the importance of our responsibility for each other. I will distinguish two kinds of responsibility: the one will be called 'linear', to denote our responsibility for what we have done; the other will be called 'lateral', to denote our responsibility for each other. Both, and not just the second, are part of our interdependent responsibility: persons not responsible for themselves and their actions can hardly be capable of responsibility for others. However, because we are not merely self-contained and isolated entities—since this would be contrary to the necessary interdependence of personal existence—linear responsibility is in various ways open to modification by lateral responsibility and should always be set in this broader context. The two evidently overlap. We may be responsible for having done something, on the linear principle, which involved a neglect of our duty to others. Thus, the wrongdoer's responsibility for his actions may also be interpreted as his abuse of lateral responsibility, and this reminds us that wrongdoing is to be seen within the context of interdependence.

The lateral principle may refer to a number of things in connection with wrongdoing. Its application to the wrongdoer is but one factor. The complementary aspect of this is the fact of the person wronged suffering through the abuse of the lateral principle. The lateral principle enables the wrongdoer to hurt and thus likewise the wronged to suffer. (We are interdependent, not mutually inaccessible.) However, the person wronged is not merely passive. As will later become evident, the burden inflicted *by* others can become a burden borne *for* others. This is the working of vicariousness—that is to say, working for the restoration of interdependence by the very means of interdependence. Wrongdoer and wronged are interlinked. Their paths are brought forcibly together at the point of wrongdoing, and it is important to consider the subsequent paths of both. Since there are often two parties involved in an act of wrongdoing, it is more logical to consider both rather than one alone. Little attention has hitherto been paid to the wrongdoer-wronged relation,[7] and yet the consequences of wrongdoing are not distributed one-sidedly. Moral consequences, and often material consequences, are felt by both parties, and thus the transformation of consequences is a possibility for and in wrongdoer and wronged alike.

In this way, the fact of interdependence must be reaffirmed when the question is asked why people could not have been prohibited from hurting one another in the first place. This is in any case a speculative point, reflecting on 'what might have been'—not a suggestion for action, since there is no way of implementing it. However, if by some inconceivable means people had been prevented from hurting each other—presumably by some form of mutual inaccessibility—this would also have precluded the *choice* of doing good to each other. If, as is generally agreed, personal goodness requires the choice of the agent, the *possibility* of choice must be available. For this one requires interdependence, not inaccessibility. Either one has interdependence, or one does not have it; one cannot opt for good-relatedness without the *possibility* of bad-relatedness. Interdependence is the one basis for personal existence and anything else, even if linguistically conceivable, would seem to be a logical impossibility. Thus, the way to prevent people from hurting each other is not by ruling out the possibility of this hurting, since this would be to rule out all else besides. The need is to actualize the proper use of interdependence, realizing one possibility rather than the other; which *in fact* would just as effectively prevent people from hurting each other as would the theoretical prevention of this possibility in the first place.

As a corollary to this, it would not seem strictly logical to use the 'freewill defence' to answer the question 'Why do the innocent suffer?' It may be an answer to the prior question 'Why do people cause suffering?' This is effectively the first question to be asked, but to answer it is to preclude the need to ask the second question, since the causation of suffering, by the one party, of itself implies the undergoing of suffering, by the other party. This does not of course cover the kind of innocent suffering not caused by human agency, but within the scope of the given inquiry it does elucidate which question belongs to which answer, which is also of value.

Moreover, the question 'Why do people cause suffering?' is not only part of the discussion of suffering, but also refers to sin. It is hard to avoid linking the two in this kind of discussion since so much, though evidently not all, of the problem of suffering is connected with the problem of sin. And suffering itself is not solely a matter of physical evil. It can be that, but of greater interest for our purposes is suffering understood in moral terms—that is, in terms of moral good and evil, for in the ethical sphere suffering does not refer to evil alone, but also to penitential suffering or the pain of conscience that is involved in the restoration to goodness. It is questions both of moral evil and of moral good that we must deal with.

We are linked, for better or for worse. This is the crux of the matter. People can help others and be helped by them. People can hurt others and be hurt by them. We are both active and passive in relation to each other. The central point is that we are not mutually inaccessible, and it is the working out of our mutual accessibility which is presupposed by the discussion of sin and suffering. The goal is not the cessation of sin and suffering *per se*, but the restoration of interdependence, between man and God and man and man. The methods used towards this must not be self-defeating; if they ignore the given presupposition, of interdependence, they may frustrate the end desired. Such a word as 'salvation' is itself ambivalent, and may be used of goals incompatible with the framework of interdependence. The word best descriptive of the Christian, interdependent understanding of salvation is 'vicariousness', where the lateral principle is unambiguously clear.

Kenosis or self-emptying is *in itself* a feature of interdependence. It is vitally important to realize this. Interdependence abused is traumatic, but interdependence upheld is dynamic, not static, and requires constant 'maintenance'. It is the *cessation* of self-giving which is the breakdown of interdependence. The restoration of interdependence involves the restoration of self-giving. (Innocent) suffering may be the form taken by interdependence in a sinful world, but self-emptying in itself is a feature of interdependence as such. It is not an innovation or mutation necessitated by the abuse of interdependence. Hence, in the restoration of interdependence suffering may cease, but one will still be emptied to the depths.

What of the question of human suffering vis-à-vis God? It will be seen that, on the understanding of human interdependence, the emphasis here will be on the injustice of man as responsible for suffering—the known injustice of man, rather than the postulated injustice of God. One might, of course, wish to take the argument a stage further back and ask why God created man in such a way that he is capable of injustice. However, this is the very question we have already considered. It is not primarily a matter of man being capable of injustice. It is a matter of man being interdependent. We have said that interdependence is the only possible basis for personal existence, and it includes within itself the twofold possibility, to help or to hurt.

In practice it must be admitted that the indictment of man has continued to provide a powerful argument for the rejection of theodicy, as is particularly evident in literary discussion. In *The Brothers Karamazov*, Dostoevsky has Ivan Karamazov insist that innocent suffering actually *should* not be justified.[8] He admits the possibility of a final harmony, but does not want it: the price is too high. Ivan's position is humanist without actually being atheist. God's existence is accepted; God's world is not. However, this somewhat anti-theistic stance may readily be taken a stage further, as in the thought of Albert Camus. The two major themes of his writings are *l'absurde* and *la révolte*, which in effect denote man's situation and man's proper response to his situation. Camus saw himself as 'an optimist on the value of man and a pessimist on his destiny'.[9] He passionately opposes a view of the universe that seems to condone the innocent suffering of children.[10] The universe as it is is unacceptable. There is to be no resignation in the face of evil—even suicide would be merely to cancel one's protest—and for Camus the fight against evil will be the stronger and more deliberate if one does not believe in God.

The atheistic, and certainly the anti-theistic, positions may begin by defining themselves in contrast to the theistic position. However, when theodicy has been rejected, the *theoretical* problem of suffering must be altered, at any rate for the atheist, for whom there is no God to be part of the data of the problem of suffering. The impact of suffering as a human and existential problem may well arouse acute concern, but the intellectual position supporting this concern has to be different. Thus it may be considered that theodicy articulates only one form of the problem of suffering, since suffering remains problematical even when there is no belief in God.

It is clear, too, that the rejection of (the acceptability of) theodicy is not tantamount to the abolition of suffering. The 'removal' of God may for some prove to be a solution to the philosophical difficulties involved in theodicy, but the theoretical adjustment of the problem does not dispose of the problematic phenomenon as such. One may choose, in the face of suffering, not to believe in God or, as an anti-theist, to oppose him; but when the choice is made, you still remain face to face with suffering. The presence of God may be regarded as an alleviation of the problem, or as its aggravation: it may be considered that a consistent intellectual position may be built on either basis. What would not be logical would be to keep on changing one's belief as to the existence of God on the basis of one's varying attitudes towards suffering. If God exists, he exists; if he does not, he does not. He cannot, as it were, be wished into and out of existence as a corollary to our changing feelings about suffering. It is not the existence of God, but our relationship with him, that would be affected in this way.

Be this as it may, traditional theodicy still requires an ongoing reappraisal. Often the statement is made that, 'If God is all-good and all-powerful, there should be no evil.' This is a summary statement and ought not to be seen as fully definitive, since it certainly is not such. There are too many hidden factors, which are not explicit in the statement. We will suggest some of these points.

The term 'all-powerful' or omnipotent does not have to include omniscience, though it does not necessarily exclude it either. It is important that omniscience should be explicitly mentioned, since in its absence an obvious objection springs to mind: one may be fully able and willing to do something, but does one know what ought to be done? On the human level the need for this third term can be clearly seen, when one reflects on how much harm has inadvertently been caused through sheer ignorance or insensitivity. To be able and willing is not enough by itself. One must acknowledge the need for the third factor, and for clarity's sake bring it into the statement of theodicy. Thus, the clause should read: 'If God is all-good and all-powerful *and* all-knowing ...' This latter is a typical hidden factor.

Again, if God *is* (all-good, all-powerful, all-knowing), the first corollary is not in fact that there should be no evil. A prior implication is that there should be nothing else *at all*. Pantheism is perhaps more strictly logical than monotheism in this respect. If God *is* (infinite, in whatever terms this may be expressed), there is no reason to assume that there should be anything else besides God. Indeed, logically speaking, this might seem to be a sheer impossibility! Yet, it *is so*. There is the creation, as well as the infinite God. One takes the leap necessary to reach this assumption because the empirical evidence for the existence of created beings is so overwhelming. God is not alone-existing, and yet we tend to take for granted this incredible paradox of all paradoxes. We say that there should logically be no evil, and forget that there should logically be nothing at all besides God anyway. Thus, once we have granted one 'logical impossibility' (namely, the existence of things besides God), we need not be so dogmatic in asserting what else is impossible. This is not to say that we are misguided in seeing evil as problematic; but to assert that it is problematic is a completely different thing from asserting that it is impossible. It is in any case pointless to assert that something is impossible when it has actually happened.

More specifically, it is not just a question of other things besides God existing, though this is the primary paradox. We have also asserted that God is all-powerful. Yet we do not see this as incompatible with the assertion that we have some power. The omnipotence of God is not taken to preclude the limited potencies of human persons, though this too may be considered remarkable. Likewise, we too have some knowledge, while God is taken to be omniscient. And the same point may be made in connection with other characteristics—even of goodness, though here some may wish to say that all goodness is of God, and that human goodness must be spoken of in these terms. However, the point may be adequately made with the preceding illustrations. Thus, we have further instances of hidden factors, and the first clause of the statement may again be expanded, to read: 'If God is all-good, all-powerful and all-knowing, and if it is accepted that other things genuinely exist besides God, and that some of these may without contradiction (i.e. without prejudice to the first part of this statement) be said to be good, powerful and knowing . . .'

We may also qualify what has just been said by a closer examination of what is implied by goodness. It has already been asserted that goodness should be seen, not as something abstract, but within the context of interdependence. Thus, if we apply the term 'good' to created beings, we should remind ourselves that this implies that a being created interdependent has chosen to take up the option of good. The given person is only secondarily to be described as good or evil; primarily he is to be described as interdependent, with the twofold possibility of acting for good or for ill. And, once interdependence is specifically brought into the statement of theodicy, it becomes less difficult to see how the second clause, about evil, may be actualized. If goodness cannot be separated from interdependence (though it is not identical with it), then this also implies that it cannot be separated from the *possibility* of evil. If the problem is articulated solely in terms of good and evil—along the lines of 'If good, why evil?'—the two terms are bound to be seen as completely irreconcilable. But if one speaks in terms of interdependence, one shows the relation between the two possibilities, while not minimizing the colossal difference in quality between them. This does not result in rendering evil as such less mysterious; but it does reshape the question we ask, and thus the inquiry is furthered.

An alternative statement of the problem of theodicy, often met with, runs like this: 'Why did God create the world like this?' At first sight, this might seem to be a question equivalent to the previous statement. (If God is all-good and all-powerful, etc., there should be no evil.) It presupposes the same qualities about God, certainly. But then it becomes more specific, in that it focuses on creation—and here a new factor, or rather presupposition, is introduced. The past tense is used ('did . . . create'), and the emphasis is entirely retrospective. But is this the only possible perspective? The world is in existence, and therefore one may fairly say that creation has at least been begun—but is one entitled to assume that it has been completed also? It might be possible to hypothesize that the world is still in the process of being created, that it is still developing and has not yet reached its final stage or 'adulthood'. In this case the question might be asked: 'Why *is* God creating the world like this?' This is perhaps no less problematic as a question, but it does shift the perspective, and suggests also that a final answer may not be available as yet. By contrast the previous formulation of the problem suggests that there must be an answer already available, since the action inquired about is presumed to have long been in a state of completion.

This possible shift in perspective is not straightforwardly the distinction between the Augustinian and Irenaean types of theodicy.[11] The Augustinian type is retrospective, formulating theodicy by an appeal to the past. The Irenaean type, as prospective, looks for some ultimate resolution of the problem in the future. But both presuppose creation as a past and completed fact, the former treating it as essential to the data of theodicy, the latter regarding it as irrelevant to its solution. However, if the world might be understood as still in the process of creation, it would be possible to adopt a prospective theodicy which nevertheless regarded creation (to be completed in the future) as essential to its formulation of the solution. Herein it differs from the typical Augustinian/Irenaean distinction, though drawing elements from each approach. This may be termed the 'ontogenetic' view, the chief contemporary representative of which is Teilhard de Chardin.

Theodicy as it is usually stated tends to be theistic rather than distinctively Christian. This needs to be taken into account when seeking a specifically Christian answer to the questions involved. Two points in particular may be taken as distinctively Christian modifications of the statement of theodicy. First, there is the understanding of interdependence or coinherence, arising from the uniquely Christian understanding of God as One-in-Trinity, a monotheism that is not unitarianism. The Christian evaluation of theodicy has not taken this sufficiently seriously hitherto, but the understanding of God and of man that is implicit in this should in turn influence the approach to such a problem as theodicy.

Second, how far has the question raised in theodicy met its answer in the atonement, which is so central to Christianity? At the very least, it would seem that much of the data involved in theodicy must now be transferred to the framework of the atonement. Or rather, it *has been* transferred. Since Christ *has* acted, the possibility or necessity of atonement cannot any longer be a matter of hypothesis, even if its outworking is yet to be fully achieved. This is vital to bear in mind.

There are, of course, a number of different emphases in theodicy and in atonement respectively, and thus the transfer of data is not entirely straightforward. Moreover, even for Christians theodicy is still a question raised and discussed—it has not been entirely subsumed to atonement, or rendered redundant as a valid question. What of the relation between theodicy and atonement?

Interdependence features in both theodicy and atonement. Much, though not all, innocent suffering is caused by man against man. In this way theodicy presupposes the abuse of interdependence, and implies some concern for moral evil as well as for physical evil. The atonement seeks the restoration of interdependence. Moreover, it can use the methods of interdependence in order to reach its goal. Innocent suffering, which in theodicy is integral to the problem, may in atonement be taken up into the solution also. There is the possibility of vicariousness: innocent suffering can be used, by God and by man, for the sake of man. Thus, while theodicy searches for the possible meaning of innocent suffering, the atonement may actually make use of it and give it some value. Theodicy asks '*Why* is it so?' The atonement gives an answer of *how* to deal with it. Theodicy is more concerned with the origin and the explanation. The concern in atonement is for reaching a practical solution—dealing with the given problem takes priority over the provision of explanations, though these are certainly not precluded. Theodicy focuses on suffering, even though much suffering does presuppose sin, and therefore calls for consideration of sin also. The atonement focuses on sin and moral evil, but also gives scope for the consideration of most kinds of suffering. It attempts to deal with the effect primarily by dealing with the cause (sin), whereas theodicy perhaps focuses too largely on the effect (suffering, instead of sin as causative of much of suffering) and requires to be complemented by the insights of atonement. Theodicy may see the cessation of suffering as the primary goal; but without the restoration of interdependence, it is quite probably self-defeating to attempt to seek deliverance from suffering. When interdependence is restored, suffering may as a corollary be done away with, or at any rate be totally transformed. However, since interdependence is itself the reciprocity of mutual self-giving, the ending of suffering is not to be confused—as it so readily is—with the possibility of a blissfully undemanding self-containedness. This would be totally contrary to interdependence, which finds its fulfilment in total self-emptying—the constant, voluntary, exhausting but life-giving dynamic of love.

## 2

# The Creator and his Creation

Kenosis—the self-emptying and self-giving that is love's essential quality—is above all to be understood as characteristic of the life of God, in that God is made known to us as love. The coinherence or *perichoresis* or mutual indwelling of the Trinity may itself be defined as a constant act of kenosis. In this way kenosis may be seen as involved in the very being of God. Only secondarily is it a mark of God's action vis-à-vis created being.

Creation itself is an act of kenosis, in that the uncreated and infinite God allows there to be beings besides himself. We have already pointed out how the existence of created beings is one of the paradoxes of monotheism. Pantheism obviates the paradox by a more strictly logical insistence that nothing else can exist besides the infinite God. It will not recognize the possibility of voluntary self-limitation, although this denial itself limits the sovereign capacity of God, in that it is insisted that God cannot choose to act thus. However, it is part of the Christian faith to accept that the sovereign God has chosen to become the creator God, i.e. God who allows there to be other beings besides himself, fundamentally dependent on himself but not 'part' of him. Moreover, some of these created beings are given the specific capacity for a personal relationship with God. God's act of kenosis in creation not merely allows for existence other than himself, but actually gives man, as created being, the possibility of choosing the relationship that will be his fulfilment (it would not be a genuine personal relationship if there were no possibility of choice). But man may in fact not choose this. Man has freedom of choice—not in the sense that there are two equal options to choose from, but that the one option that is life and fulfilment for man cannot be forced on him against his will, but must be chosen (and therefore may be not chosen). This is not to say that man's effort is all that counts. God's love always has the priority. But man will not be saved *against* his will; in some sense there is need for 'consent' or 'response'. Man's freedom is, properly, freedom to choose life, in relationship with God. Freedom is not the multiplicity of options, but the voluntary response of love to love, of man's love to God's love. Somehow, however, this freedom has not been fulfilled: man has found himself in a situation of estrangement, involving enslavement to the things that tend to the disintegration and ultimate death of personal being. God's act of kenosis in creation was to allow man 'room' for the choice of life. Since this choice was not fulfilled, the creator God took upon himself an even more costly act of kenosis. Christ, who is God of God, emptied himself[1] and was made incarnate.

> When (Christ) was incarnate and made man, he summed up in himself the long line of the human race, securing for us all ... salvation, so that we should regain in Christ Jesus what we had lost in Adam, namely, being in the image and likeness of God.[2]

In this action of the creator towards his creation, which is known as redemption, we shall take as our primary frame of reference the thought of St Irenaeus, second-century bishop of Lyons. Characteristic of St Irenaeus' approach is the idea, derived from St Paul,[3] that Christ 'recapitulates' human nature. Christ was

> God *summing up anew* in himself the old formation of man, that he might slay sin, abolish death, and give life to man.[4]

God who created us also acted to re-create or redeem us, that is, to restore his purpose for us and our relationship with him. At the same time this was done by a complete act of solidarity with mankind. Christ became truly human, and as man recapitulated the whole human experience. God not only created man in his image and likeness but in Christ fulfilled that same image and likeness *in himself*, as human. The restoration was not a merely 'external' act, by God vis-à-vis man, but something personally appropriated, by God *as* man.

> ... he ... truly revealed the image, himself having become that very thing which the image of him was.[5]

Christ took upon himself the whole human situation and shared it in everything. It might be said that Christ's birth as man was the *beginning* of the incarnation. The idea underlying 'recapitualation' is that of 'analogy' or 'going over the ground again'. Thus, for the restoration and perfection of human nature *all* of Christ's human experience is important. We are to understand Christ's sinlessness in a dynamic way, in terms of his obedience. Christ's humanity was not an untested innocence, but fully tested and proven.[6] Exemption from temptation and the need for decision would *ipso facto* have meant disengagement from the very conflict Christ was undertaking on our behalf. The incarnation involved the continuing *choice* of obedience, the consent of moral personality. Following St Paul, St Irenaeus constantly emphasizes how Christ's obedience is to counterbalance our disobedience: '... being as he was a man ... and by obedience paying the debt of disobedience'.[7] Christ's obedience —the constant reponsiveness of his self-emptying—is essential to the recapitulation of human nature, in that obedience is to be understood as definitive of true humanity. Obedience is the union of man's will with God's will, and so itself is the fulfilment of human life according to the intention of its creation. Sin or disobedience may not rightly be called normal for humanity. It is essentially unnatural, since it is in no way definitive of man's true nature, which is to be according to the image and likeness of God.

> ... it is good to obey God, and to believe him, and to keep his commandment: and this is the life of man: even as not to obey God is bad; and this is man's death.[8]

St Irenaeus has much to say about life and incorruption, which Christ gives to humanity, and it is clear that life is to be understood in ethical and not merely biological terms. Life and obedience and relationship with God are linked together; similarly disobedience, wilful separation from God, and disruption in relationship are linked with death.[9] God as creator is by this fact the only source of life. Man does not have life of himself, but only from God.[10] To share in the life of God,[11] in union with him, *is* man's life; and redemption is the restoration of this life-giving relationship. Thus, we are 'made by him who has power to give incorruption to be after his own likeness'.[12]

Through the incarnation the creator recapitulates his creation. Humanity may be the focal point of this, but creation in its entirety is to be understood as involved. St Paul spoke of God's purpose as being that 'the universe, all in heaven and on earth, might be brought into a unity in Christ'[13]. Following this, St

Irenaeus says that Christ has summed up the old work of creation in himself,[14] and that 'the creation ... itself must be renewed to its old condition, and without hindrance serve the righteous'.[15]

It is important to bear in mind that God created the whole world and not just man. Thus he seeks to redeem the whole world, his whole creation, and not man alone. To realize this will in fact affect even our understanding of the redemption of man. The material world is to be redeemed; it is not to be redeemed *from*. Man is to be delivered, not from materiality, but from sin and evil. To adopt a dualism of matter and spirit leads to a lack of appreciation of matter in itself, and thus of God as the creator of matter; and denies the ethical seriousness of evil, and hence also of the kind of measures to be taken to combat it. Salvation is not release from matter, or 'dematerialization'. Christ, the Word of God, became *flesh*.[16] His solidarity did not stop short of this material involvement, but was truly *incarnation*.

In his writings St Irenaeus strongly resisted the inroads of dualistic gnosticism into second-century Christianity. The Christian understanding both of creation and of redemption would—as just indicated—have been undermined by the admission of dualism. The gnostic ideology as such may no longer be with us, but the temptation to dualism, with its various corollaries, is a perennial one. In place of an explicit dualism there is, for instance, the widespread tendency to neglect the significance of the material world. Man alone is seen as important, though in this it may be forgotten that man himself is a 'material' being and is closely involved with the rest of the material creation. This may perhaps be termed dualism by default. Second, there is the danger of practical neglect and exploitation of the material world, consequent on the absence of a suitable theoretical appreciation of it. Yet man ought not to enslave or be enslaved by the material creation, and both man and the rest of creation are to be restored to their true position vis-à-vis God who created them. The *whole* creation is to be understood as the object of God's creative and re-creative care. Thus, for man the concern for technology and ecology are not theologically insignificant, but should arise naturally from man's understanding of his position vis-à-vis both his creator and the rest of creation. And man's responsibility for the rest of creation should be enhanced and not diminished in man's own restoration.

Another gnostic tendency is the subversion of monotheism by a theoretical or practical ditheism. It is important to emphasize that our redeemer is none other than our creator. The redeemer God redeems what is already, in a most fundamental sense, *his own*. His concern and responsibility for us do not originate at the point of redemption. Indeed if God our redeemer did not also create us, he could not be sovereign, the one God. Contemporary thought would not specifically postulate two different 'gods', one for creation and one for redemption. In practice, though, there is an implicit dichotomy between the theology of creation and the theology of redemption. It may be said, for instance, that the Christian faith concerns our redemption. This is true, but risks being reduced to a half-truth if it is not borne in mind that redemption itself is re-creation—the restoration of creation to what God its creator has intended for it. Christ recapitulated or summed up in himself 'not some other creation, but the original one'.[17] Likewise, we are to 'arrive at *the old nature of man* ... which was made in God's image and likeness'.[18] It is the theology of creation that provides the perspective for understanding the presuppositions and the goal of redemption. Thus, the re-creation of man leads not to an alien destiny but to the true fulfilment of humanity, which is the fulfilment of God's purposes for humanity.

'We who by nature belonged to God Almighty were ... alienated contrary to nature.'[19] What is natural for man is to be in communion with God, the creature with its creator. Sin is in no way natural to human life even if—tragically—it has happened to be the general condition of humanity. Man's 'natural condition' should most properly refer to man's relationship with God. It is an inversion of priorities to speak of the abnormality of sin and estrangement as man's natural condition, when in fact it is quite the contrary of this. The words 'nature' and 'natural' have been seriously devalued in theological usage. What is *natural* for the creation is to fulfil the purposes of its creator.

Granted this, there will remain a certain inevitable ambivalence in the use of the term 'natural'. Natural theology, which may be defined as the language of the theology of creation, is a distinct theological method which is to be complemented by the use of the theology of redemption. God's original purposes for his creation are only truly known and fulfilled in the restoration of these purposes. Short of this they may be partially known, in that the creation is not without 'traces' of the creator. St Paul testifies to this understanding of theology:

> ... all that may be known of God by men lies plain before their eyes; indeed God himself has disclosed it to them. His invisible attributes ... have been visible, ever since the world began, to the eye of reason, in the things he has made.[20]

The relation between the two theologies may be one of the partial or potential to the fulfilled, at any rate as far as the data to which they refer are concerned. Alternatively, the two may be contrasted as languages, differing according to the presence or absence of distinctively 'Christian' terminology—this being the specific language of the theology of redemption. To wish to make use of both methods is not to minimize the centrality of the theology of redemption of re-creation, but only to assert that it is not to be isolated from the theology of creation. Conversely, the safeguard for the use of natural theology is its link with the theology of redemption, which is to act as a control. It is above all from the perspective of redemption, rather than from outside it, that we may attempt to make some use of natural theology. One might add that ultimately the two perspectives should coincide, precisely because the theology of redemption speaks of what is most truly natural for the created order. Short of the fulfilment of restoration there does of course remain an eschatological tension between the life of the Kingdom of God and all that is not yet within this. This has to be taken into account in using natural theology, which may not merely conform to 'things as they are'. But, as the language of the theology of creation, it is a valid language for Christian use. To deny this would be to risk denying that the God of our redemption is none other than the God who created us.

However, we shall need to remember that there are two kinds of discontinuity between the creation and its creator. There is the 'gap' of sinfulness and estrangement, which is to be overcome; and there is the 'gap' between the finite and the infinite, the created and the uncreated, which will always remain. Man is not simply fallen, but also finite. Hence our theology must be subject to the awareness of an abiding discontinuity. Man is to share in the life of God, in relationship with him, but he cannot become 'part' of God. There are, and always will be, the two categories, so to speak, of created and uncreated. Moreover, it would be misleading to speak of an intermediate category of supernatural. The only contrast that should be drawn is within the category of the created: between the created in relationship with its creator—which is truly *natural*; and the created outside of its proper relationship—which is highly *unnatural*. The goal is the realization of creature-hood, or the norm of created being. The knowledge of God, or theology, becomes true within the relationship with him, in which we learn to know God, rather than just to know *about* God. It is the restoration of this relationship that is our life and redemption.

Our study will explore both man's estrangement and its consequences, and all that in creation and in re-creation tends to restoration. Thus, our approach will be informed by a twofold dialectic: much of what is said will use the language of the theology of creation, without making specific reference to re-creation or using the language of the theology of redemption. For example, we shall speak of penitence both as a general human phenomenon and also as a specific characteristic of the Christian life. In both instances, and not just the latter, it is to be understood as being within the purposes of God. However, it is within the relationship with Christ that the given reality finds its fulfilment. The theology of redemption is admittedly our constant perspective, but—as itself involving the restoration of creation—it will justify the use of the language of the theology of creation. The theology of redemption will be reintroduced in specific terms only when sufficient use has been made of the natural theology that it presupposes. It is through the use of this twofold dialectic that we shall attempt to consider the ways in which the creator seeks to restore his creation.

'He became what we are, that he might make us what he is.'[21]

In considering redemption, there are two aspects to be taken into account. What Christ did, he did *for us*, and a balanced doctrine of redemption should do justice to this fact. The very nature of redemption demands that there be some response on the part of the person who receives it. In practice, the tendency is to stop short of this and to consider the work of Christ in abstraction. Arguably, however, a complete account of the doctrine of the atonement will consider both the person and work of Christ *and* what is effected by this. Christ became as we are, *that he might make us as he is*. This statement of Irenaeus is reiterated by subsequent writers for a number of centuries, and may be considered a characteristic patristic emphasis.[22] What we see in St Irenaeus is of general application. Christ's work, and its outworking and appropriation, are to be linked and not dichotomized. This should be a statement of the obvious, but in fact has proved a source of difficulty. For instance, consideration of Christian life and spirituality has often been regarded as an 'optional extra', and discussion of redemption has been regarded as complete with little or no attention given to this. Alternatively, atonement theory has sometimes been divided into two categories, objective and subjective, and in this way the two complementary aspects of redemption have been seen as mutually exclusive alternatives. But both aspects are important. We have already spoken of how 'he became what we are'. We shall now discuss the corollary to this, 'that he might make us what he is'.

It is generally considered that Peter Abelard (1079–1142) is the father of the so-called 'subjective' theory of the atonement, otherwise known as the exemplary theory or theory of moral influence. This is intended to indicate that stress is laid on the atonement as effected in man; and that it is the example provided by Christ, or the sight of what he has done for us, that effects this. But does this do justice to Abelard's own approach, as distinct from the approach of recent liberal thought, which would claim Abelard as its progenitor?

To begin with, we may question the desirability of using an epithet such as 'subjective'. This suggests *mere* subjectivity, and may imply the absence of anything objective. In terms of atonement theory, the change that takes place in man may be given prominence at the expense of minimizing the work of Christ. But is this imbalance necessary? If we speak of 'personal appropriation' instead of 'subjectivity', we may more readily see that stress on the change in man should in no way derogate from the work of Christ, but should rather be seen as its natural corollary. If Abelard speaks of love kindled in man, it is always a *responsive* love, aroused by what Christ has done, and not otherwise.[23] Thus, we should not speak of Abelard's approach as

> ... an attempt to set the ethical, manward aspect of Atonement in a primary and not in a secondary place.[24]

Still less should we see Abelard as the founder of a theological tradition in which

> ... the Atonement is no longer regarded as in any true sense carried out by God. Rather, the Reconciliation is the result of some process that takes place in man, such as conversion and amendment.[25]

The fact that reconciliation will include conversion and amendment should not be taken to imply that the change in man is to be detached from what God has done to bring about this change. Change in man is not an *alternative* to the action of God, as the subjective theory is taken to imply. What Abelard does is to speak of both aspects of redemption—what Christ has done, and how this works out in human lives. He does not give the exceptional prominence to the latter aspect that his critics tend to assume. One might hazard the suggestion that this apparent overemphasis is detected only when it is assumed that the outworking of the atonement is not an integral part of atonement theory. However, what is being contended here is that the twofold approach of Abelard may be justified by an appeal to the patristic balance. In this respect his perspective is no innovation.

What may be designated as subjective in Abelard is not any supposed dislocation of atonement theory, but rather his genuine stress on the internal in his approach to ethics. The locus of good and evil is in the personality, not in deeds as such:

> Thus it is in the will, and not in deeds, which are common to good and bad alike, that all merit resides.[26]

And

> (God) considers the mind rather than the action when it comes to a reward, and an action adds nothing to merit whether it proceeds from a good or a bad will.[27]

Moreover, neither desire nor will by themselves add up to sin.[28] The constituent feature of sin is, in Abelard's radical definition, consent and consent alone:

> The doing of deeds has no bearing upon an increase of sin and nothing pollutes the soul except what is of the soul, that is, the consent which alone we have called sin, not the will which precedes it nor the doing of the deed which follows.[29]

Sin as thus defined is still at the same time seen in specifically theological terms:

> Now this consent we properly call sin, that is, the fault of the soul by which it earns damnation or is made guilty before God. For what is that consent unless it is contempt of God and an offence against him? ... And so our sin is contempt of the Creator and to sin is to hold the Creator in contempt, that is, to do by no means on his account what we believe we ought to do for him, or not to forsake on his account what we believe we ought to forsake.[30]

The significance of all this ethical discourse lies in its potential for interpreting Abelard's approach to the atonement. It is not, in its given form, specifically presented as a part of his atonement theory. However, it does allow us to know in some detail Abelard's mind on sin and repentance. Moreover, its emphasis on interiorization may well be linked with Abelard's statements on the effects within human personality of what Christ has done. It is hardly surprising that personal transformation should be stressed by someone for whom the whole question of sin and virtue is to be focused in the personality. The inwardness of sin calls for a corresponding inwardness of the effects of redemption. Just as consent is the definitive feature of sin, so also inward sorrow for sin is definitive of repentance.[31] But this is not to imply that our repentance may be isolated from the work of Christ. For Abelard, repentance is not autonomous but always a responsive quality, elicited by the love of God which kindles an answering love in us. It is 'a repentance to which the love of God is urging us'[32] and ...

> Those who repent healthily ... are moved to compunction less by fear of penalties than by love of him.[33]

The link between repentance and the love of God which is made in his ethics may be borne in mind when we turn again to Abelard's specific comments on redemption. In this latter context he does not do more than speak in general terms of the love that is kindled within us. He does not at this point enlarge on its moral import, but we may not for this reason assume that he sees love as devoid of ethical effect. We may hope to gauge the tendency of his thought here from what is discussed elsewhere in his writings.

The love of God, acting for our redemption, arouses love within us. But ought this to imply that Abelard's view of Christ's work is merely 'exemplarist ... excluding ... the sacrificial aspect of Calvary'?[34] The given material would not seem to justify this view. Abelard constantly stresses the costliness of Christ's love, who gives everything, to the point of giving his life for us. It is in the total gift of self that there lies the reality of sacrifice. This understanding of the sacrificial meaning of love is underlined by Abelard's favourite scriptural citation, St John 15.13: 'There is no greater love than this, that a man should lay down his life for his friends.'[35] Christ died for us,[36] while we were yet sinners,[37] and he did so out of love of us.[38] All the sufferings of the martyrs are as nothing compared to his passion, which he underwent for love of us.[39] Abelard ought hardly to be accused of neglecting reference to the death of Christ; nor does he allow love to be presented as less than utterly costly. One might suggest that this kind of understanding is better described as kenotic rather than exemplarist. At the same time, the very fact that Abelard takes love and the cost of love seriously, suggests the depth of his understanding of the situation of sin from which mankind needs redemption. Sin not only is contempt of God,[40] but actually separates us from him.[41] For this very reason Christ came to save us. And—as it is repeatedly emphasized—our redemption cost Love everything.

Abelard does not, however, consider the death of Christ in isolation. He retains a patristic emphasis on the incarnation, which in fact he links closely with the passion.[42] Both the taking up, and the laying down, of Christ's life are an act of love towards us; neither is seen in isolation, but they are linked together. There is some limited reference to Christ teaching us, by word and by example.[43] Abelard also mentions Christ as the wisdom of God, being made incarnate and illuminating us by his light.[44] But he does not suggest that Christ was merely a teacher, rather than a redeemer, as the 'moral example' theory might suggest. Teaching receives only limited mention. His major theme is the redemptive love of Christ, which involved his giving his life for us.

What Christ did for us did not simply *show* the love of God; it *was* the love of God, acting for our redemption, giving itself in everything—and seeking a response of love. Christ died for us 'that love might be spread abroad in our hearts.'[45] His life and his death bound us more closely to himself through love.[46] His passion was 'to show what love he had for man, and to stir man the more to his love'.[47] Love is understood as efficacious and not merely revelatory. Abelard typically summarizes this 'effect' by speaking of love kindled within us. He also specifically adduces the ideas of deliverance from sin, and freedom. The use of these latter ought not simply to be attributed to a desire to be faithful to the text on which he is commenting, namely, the Epistle to the Romans. That his use is appropriation, and not quotation, may be surmised from the way in which he reiterates these ideas, both here and elsewhere, and adapts them to his own characteristic emphasis. Deliverance from the enslavement of sin is linked with the outpouring of Christ's love on man.[48] And the liberty of the children of God is seen as the liberty of love.[49] Christ's work and our response are constantly linked, and indeed this response in us is spoken of as the purpose of Christ's work.[50]

It is important that, in considering love as generated within us, we should do justice to the depth already seen in Abelard's understanding of the love of Christ. It is insufficient to say that Abelard sees the cross as 'a mere incentive to love, making its appeal to emotion and to feeling.[51] Abelard speaks frequently of love, but nowhere suggests that it is to be reduced to mere sentiment. And, if it is we who have devalued the word 'love', we are not entitled to impose our reductionist tendencies on a writer whose work does not of itself suggest them. Indeed, if for Abelard love is the supreme hallmark of the divine action—with all that this implies—it indicates a high estimation of the quality of the response thus engendered in man to designate it too as love. Nothing *less* than love is a sufficient response.

Christ's work is not merely a display, though being what it is, it undoubtedly does show his love for us, and Abelard does not hesitate to say so.[52] However, when speaking of man's response, Abelard does not make any use of the language of observation. Love is spread abroad in our hearts[53] or kindled within us.[54] Abelard is not at pains to underscore the visual suggestion in his writings. The emphasis is on Christ's redemptive love and our responsive love. This all the more suggests that the visual clue is not to be wrenched from its context or reduced to merely prosaic exemplarism. Indeed, an alternative perspective for interpretation may be suggested, one with well-established patristic and indeed scriptural roots. In St Paul we read that one day 'we shall see face to face'.[55] For St Irenaeus, this 'seeing' becomes a theme of some importance, which he uses to interpret the Christian life or the outworking of redemption. For him 'the life of man is to see God'.[56] God ...

> bestows incorruption into eternal life, which ensues unto everyone from his beholding God ... being seen, He gives life to them that see Him ... Men therefore will see God so as to live.[57]

In this correlation of vision and life, we should remember that for St Irenaeus 'life' has moral and spiritual implications, and is linked with the restoration of man's relationship with God.[58] Vision is likewise linked with love:

> ... it is love which completes the perfect man, and he who loves God is perfect, both in this world and in the future. For we never come to an end in our loving of God, but the more we shall have looked upon Him, so much the more we love Him.[59]

This is not exemplarism, but contemplation. And the emphasis of the contemplative approach generally is not on mere vision, in abstraction, but above all on both the costliness and the attractiveness of love, and on its redemptive 'effect' in human lives. The importance of such an emphasis for Abelard should already be apparent. Thus, I would like to propose that the very things that suggested exemplarism to many of Abelard's interpreters may make much better sense if understood from the perspective of this older, and ongoing, tradition. One ought not, perhaps, to suggest that Abelard is a typical representative of the contemplative approach. Much of his writing is not geared to this specific orientation. And it may be that, although he reiterates his characteristic themes, he does not develop them as fully as might be desired. What I am contending, however, is that there are certain distinctive elements in Abelard's understanding of redemption which the contemplative tradition would seem most able to do justice to. This in turn must imply that, in spite of a genuine contrast with his contemporaries, he is not to be regarded as the founder of a new theological tradition. He may not, except by misunderstanding, be associated with the 'subjective' approach. This may be to credit him with somewhat less originality, but the gain is obvious if in fact this reassessment proves to do better justice to his thought. In terms of theological history, it is being contended, first, that the interpretation placed on Abelard by his contemporary St Bernard, and by a number of more recent commentators[60] is certainly a false development. Second, that it is the patristic tradition and subsequent contemplative writers that provide a proper, and more helpful, basis for comparison and interpretation.

Such is our proposed reassessment. In conclusion, we may remind ourselves of something rather fine—one of the passages where Abelard's theological calibre and devotional capacity are well matched. It is not one of his public utterances, but may for this reason be all the more true of his understanding:

> He bought thee not with His wealth but with Himself. With His own blood He bought thee and redeemed thee. See what right He has over thee, and behold how precious thou art . . . Thou art greater than heaven, thou art greater than the world; of whom the Creator of the world is Himself become the price.[61]

# 3
# Suffering, Innocent and Guilty

It is important to consider the question of man that underlies theories of the atonement. The human situation on which the atonement impinges will be reconstructed from the basis of the question of suffering.

We tend to assume that our understanding of the problem of suffering is normative, and so we read back our questions and our answers into the discussions of other times and places. Our assumption is that everyone has been troubled by the thought of innocent suffering, simply because this is a problem for us. On consideration, this proves questionable. Even we try to explain away instances of innocent suffering by saying that the sufferer must have 'done something to deserve it', and it comes as a relief to discover in this way that a supposed case of innocent suffering is really a case of guilty suffering. This kind of explaining away is interesting in that it suggests that suffering *ought* to be explained in terms of guilty suffering, and that guilty suffering has a kind of priority over innocent suffering, as being the 'proper' kind of suffering. We do not perhaps sufficiently recognize how universal is this tendency to assume the priority of guilty suffering. In actual fact, it so predominates in the thought of some cultures that it is accepted as the only possible interpretation. All suffering is, or must be seen as, guilty suffering. The possibility of explaining away some instances may be developed into a complete system, which does not recognize any innocent suffering. Thus, our problem of (innocent) suffering may not be assumed to be normative. The recognition of the very fact of innocent suffering, let alone of its problematical nature, is not something automatic, and some systems of thought do not get beyond recognizing guilty suffering. The acknowledgement of genuinely *innocent* suffering is in fact a major intellectual and moral achievement, not something to be taken for granted.

It will be important to bear in mind the distinction between guilty suffering and innocent suffering, and not to confuse the two by explaining away the one in terms of the other.

The typical system of guilty suffering may be stated thus: 'All sin results in suffering for the wrongdoer; all suffering is a consequence of wrongdoing for the wrongdoer, i.e. guilty suffering.' Thanks to these tidy equations, neither sin nor suffering may be regarded as problematical. Both are, in an ironically literal sense, accounted for. There is no surplus, no absurdity. In this 'equation theory' all suffering is one's own suffering—one has brought it on oneself, and one bears it in one's own person, i.e. for oneself. The implications of this are particularly interesting. By stating that all suffering is one's own, deserved suffering, it precludes not merely innocent suffering but also the possibility of vicarious suffering. The Christian faith would consider vicarious suffering— suffering for and on behalf of others—to be a valid and valuable possibility. However, this is not only omitted from consideration but is actually inconceivable in the terms of such a scheme. If all suffering is and must be one's own suffering, this implies (a) that since there can be only guilty suffering, there is by definition no such thing as innocent suffering; (b) that if one can only suffer for oneself, one *cannot* suffer for others. Vicarious suffering is incompatible with systems of guilty suffering. This is not to make innocent suffering in itself less unpalatable, nor can one straightforwardly translate innocent suffering into vicariousness. But innocent suffering does prove to be the necessary basis for the possibility of vicarious suffering.

In any case, is the equation theory as watertight as it seems? The wrongdoer, whose act of wrongdoing is to be followed by suffering, will in many cases have *caused* suffering by his act of wrongdoing. If—as would seem probable—we are to interpret this as the causation of innocent suffering, the equation theory cannot stand. Of itself it implies innocent suffering, in that it speaks of the guilty, who has caused innocent suffering. The suffering of the wrongdoer's victim is the irreducible minimum of innocent suffering which systems such as the equation theory cannot properly contain. One might attempt to get round this by supposing that the so-called victim for some reason deserved this suffering, and thus the guilty party was in effect the unwitting instrument of justice. However, even if this might be taken as plausible in some instances, it could not be accepted as a general principle, in that it would render the use of the term 'guilty' pointless. If the 'wrongdoer' is always, necessarily, the instrument of justice, in what sense may one properly speak of his guilt? If to inflict suffering on a person is by definition to requite them for their misdeeds, wherein lies the wrongful quality of the act of infliction? The infliction of suffering ought not ever to be considered a misdeed, if from the victim's point of view the infliction of suffering may only be seen as the working of justice. In practice, of course, these implications do not seem to be realized: acts of infliction are (properly, if not consistently) considered *wrong*.

Similarly, if guilt alone is possible, then one must speak of the guilty causing deserved suffering to the guilty, and being held guilty for serving as the instruments of justice. There is no room left for innocence. But with only one category available for interpretation, namely, guilt, there is no possibility of contrast, and the task of ethical judgement risks being rendered meaningless. If innocence is not possible, then neither is guilt.

As regards the discussion of responsibility, it becomes clear that this theory of guilty suffering attempts to see everything exclusively in terms of linear responsibility. If our responsibility for what we have done signifies the only kind of responsibility, it is not hard to take the further step of seeing all suffering as guilty suffering. We suffer, and can only suffer, for what we have done. In one move this attempts to preclude the possibility of both lateral responsibility and innocent suffering. Is there, moreover, any point in helping those who suffer? On the logic of the given theory, we might thereby be thwarting the process of justice! In any case, if we are genuinely free to help people, it should also be possible by that same freedom to hurt them—in the sense of causing them innocent suffering, not merely executing justice upon them. The mutual accessibility which permits genuine assistance ought also to permit genuinely detrimental actions. An exclusively linear model is insufficient for the interpretation of experience.

The equation theory is also subject to a major difficulty which becomes evident when one attempts to see how it may work out in practice. The besetting problem of this kind of hypothesis is the time-factor. How can the equation theory (all sin leads to suffering for the wrongdoer; all suffering is guilty suffering) actually be worked out in the space of a given lifetime, which is in any case of no fixed length? Anticipating the unreliability of one's 'allowance' of time, it might be considered desirable for consequences to be worked through without delay, automatically. This does not happen as a general rule, and to all appearances the theory does not work out. In some instances a wrongdoer may be said to meet his due. Similarly, a given case of suffering may sometimes be correctly attributed to some antecedent wrongdoing on the part of the sufferer. But this is not an invariable rule, and it cannot be said that sooner or later these two things—sin and suffering—may always be linked in this way. And yet the demand to link them is extremely strong. Hence if the equation theory of sin and suffering is to be maintained, it tends to lead to some kind of strict formulation—that is, in terms of a time-dominated theory. The apparent nonconformity of facts to theory leads to the use of certain subsidiary hypotheses, by which it is intended that the given facts may be accommodated to the primary pattern and the major hypothesis be reinforced. If there is not enough time, let there be more time!

When the time-factor is of primary importance, there must be a guarantee of sufficient time for consequences to be fulfilled. This may be arranged in two ways in particular. Liability may be imputed to subsequent generations, by an assertion of collective responsibility for the action of one particular individual in the first generation. This is the 'nemesis pattern', which is a partial version of the equation theory and will be discussed later. Alternatively, the limitations of the time-factor may be overcome by postulating the rebirth of a given individual, in order to work through all the consequences due to him. Here there is an insistence on individual responsibility, which is made possible by an assertion of identity: 'b' is the reincarnation of 'a' and will be born again as 'c'. One may note, however, that if one does not accept the postulate of reincarnation, this scheme would appear to be yet again one of collective responsibility. Although intended to emphasize individual responsibility, in practice it could be said to detract from it, if *in fact* 'b' is not the reincarnation of 'a' and is not to be held responsible for the misdeeds of 'a'.

To designate all suffering as guilty suffering is a concession to the desire to see that the sum of suffering matches the sum of wrongdoing, thus attempting to ensure that the consequences of wrongdoing are—at least to appearances—worked out in time. However, this involves a lack of appreciation of the real import of certain instances of suffering, through the refusal to recognize innocent suffering. In addition, the handling of the concepts of personal identity and personal responsibility will to many seem strained or less than satisfactory. This kind of attempt to reinforce the equation theory is perhaps unduly subservient to the needs of the time-factor. Of course, the problem must not be denied the opportunity of solution, and the very approaches we have mentioned testify to the need to find a solution to the problem at whatever cost. The mistake is to assume that the alternative to being thwarted by the time-factor is in some way to provide more time. When time in the sense of a greater length of temporality is central to the solution of the problem, one may hesitate to speak of the problem as being genuinely resolved. Consequences are merely allowed to 'run their course', to be prolonged until exhausted. This is a primarily quantitative approach, which does not in fact sever the solution of the problem from its dependence on the time-factor. No qualitative reappraisal is undertaken.

It may of course prove impossible to escape the influence of the time-factor altogether, even if one may wish to claim that certain systems of understanding which are dominated by the time-factor are unsatisfactory as solutions to the problem. It should be noted that Christianity does accept the idea of there being time beyond a given lifetime. It will not accept the idea of reincarnation, and in so doing presumably attempts to dissociate itself from any idea of a return to merely temporal conditions. However, the Christian faith does accept 'continuation' in some sense, while attempting to divest it of purely temporal connotations. Eternal life is primarily qualitative. It can be 'there and then', but only inasmuch as it can firstly be 'here and now' and does not have to be only a subsequent condition.[1] This is not to avoid temporal reference altogether, but the temporal factor is not allowed to dominate all else. It is the emphasis that is vital.

One should not, by the way, assume that the acceptance of a theory of guilty suffering precludes all actual thought of innocent suffering. An equation theory might be the dominant theory in a given culture, but might coexist with the acceptance in practice of instances of innocent suffering. Indeed one would expect this if, as we have suggested, a linear theory is not truly self-sufficient but requires to be modified by a lateral context. This does not imply a systematized belief in both kinds of suffering. It is just that there may be some—potentially fruitful—discrepancies within an overall system of belief which theoretically excludes them.

We shall examine in some detail what is perhaps the clearest and most interesting example of an equation theory: the system of karma. This is particularly characteristic of the Hindu-Buddhist approach, though karmic elements are to be found elsewhere as well. Here we shall speak of karma from the Buddhist standpoint.

In terms of the preceding discussion this system is an equation theory which uses the subsidiary hypothesis of reincarnation in order to satisfy the requirements of the time-factor. Karma of itself may be defined in some such terms as 'action-reaction'. However, just as the requirements of the equation theory cannot usually be worked out in a single lifetime, so similarly karma requires the corollary of rebirth for its basic postulate to attain realization. Thus, any given individual has been born prior to this lifetime, and so his present suffering betokens previous wrongdoing. And in addition he will be reborn subsequent to this lifetime, in order that any current wrongdoing or unexpiated entail may receive its due. Karma is not itself rebirth and could in theory be detached from rebirth. But this would not work in practice, and so practical requirements have led to the acceptance of this particular corollary. The extension of time is essential to the solution. Consequences are due to one for certain actions, and they are to run their course until exhausted. Rebirth is determined by an unexhausted karma.

As a system of consequences karma may refer not only to misdeeds but to all deeds, good and bad alike. However, the chief emphasis is on misdeeds, and the accumulation and working-through of consequences due to misdeeds. Guilty suffering is the only type of suffering recognized. The sufferer is *ipso facto* a wrongdoer, in whom the consequences of his misdeeds are being duly worked out. Interestingly, far more emphasis is given to suffering than to sin or wrongdoing, though this is the stated cause of suffering. Suffering as the consequence of wrong is important, wrong as the cause of suffering is of relatively lesser concern. This is reflected in the approach to dealing with the given phenomenon, guilty suffering. The accumulated debt of consequences is to run its course, namely, in terms of suffering.

In addition, the attempt will be made to accumulate no more consequences to be worked through. In this way, the focus is not on sin as such or—except indirectly—on the need to tackle sin for itself. The basic premiss is the universality of suffering and the goal is that of liberation from suffering.[2] Since such suffering is understood as a consequence of wrongdoing, deliverance from it may to that extent be considered analogous to the idea of deliverance from sin. But the comparison has to be an oblique one. Despite a common presupposition—of sin or wrongdoing, which has consequences—there is a significant difference of emphasis. Deliverance from suffering, albeit guilty suffering, may not straightforwardly be equated with salvation from sin.

Buddhism treats of a problem of suffering, but clearly does so in a different manner from Christian-influenced western philosophy, in that our problem is one of innocent suffering and the Buddhist system recognizes only guilty suffering. When we speak of the problem of suffering, it is innocent suffering that we have in mind. Guilty suffering presents no comparable intellectual problem for us. Strictly speaking, it is not a *problem* for Buddhism either. It is after all explicable, as being the proper due of wrongdoing. In any case, there can be no problem of innocent suffering in Buddhism, because no such thing as innocent suffering is recognized. Buddhism does sometimes speak of suffering as a condition of temporal existence. This does not in fact prove to be a reference to innocent suffering, as distinct from guilty suffering. It is simply that persons within temporal existence are prone to involvement in the karmic process, i.e. to guilty suffering as already discussed.

Buddhism does not maintain a belief in a god, hence one ought not to speak of its approach as a kind of theodicy, which by definition must include reference to God. It shares the concern of theodicy to the extent that its focus of interest is on suffering rather than sin, but differs from it by its recognition of guilty suffering alone, whereas theodicy is based on an acknowledgement of innocent suffering. The system of karma, although comparable in some of its emphases to both theodicy and redemption, must be carefully distinguished from both of these as understood by western thought.

One is to work through one's karma and thus 'attain salvation'. The goal is one of freedom from action-reaction. What is the significance of one's personal disposition in this? At the stage of action, or the beginning of the karmic process, it is said that '... the *mind* is the maker of karma, good or bad, and hence the intention of the mind at the time of action determines the incidence of the resultant merit'.[3] Conversely, detachment enables actions to be performed without any karmic entail. But, subsequent to the commission of non-detached actions, there can be no question of merely 'willing away' their consequences. 'Only the ignorant personify Karma, and attempt to bribe, petition, or cajole it; wise men understand it and conform to it.'[4] The mind may be the maker of karma, but this latter statement suggests that it is not permitted to be its unmaker, at any rate not to such an extent as to be subversive of the basic pattern of karma. Some form of modification is possible, though. 'There is a given pattern (of karma), and to rejoice in it strengthens it, while to repent of it weakens it.'[5] However, Buddhism repudiates another type of modification which in western thought is generally considered complementary to that of repentance, namely, forgiveness. 'The karmic law merely asserts that this direction cannot be altered suddenly by the forgiveness of sins, but must be changed by our own effort.'[6] One's own disposition, and not that of others towards one, is significant for the karmic process. The linear principle is here paramount.

Despite this primarily linear model there are some signs not of the modification of the model as such, but of lateral ideas being held side by side with the primary model, though perhaps insufficiently co-ordinated with it. Karma may be expressed as a law of the universe, as well as that of any individual. 'The universe is itself an effect; hence all the units in it, viewed as events, are at once both cause and effect within a vast effect. Each is at once the result of all that has preceded it and a contributing cause of all to come.'[7] This basically expresses an inter-relation of events, rather than of persons. It might even be spoken of as a kind of interdependence of humanity, since people are the agents who perform the actions entailing the karmic process, and likewise people are the locus of the effects of this process, namely, suffering. But the interpretation of this inter-relation seems to be essentially impersonal. Significantly, it is not permitted to modify the understanding of all suffering being guilty suffering: suffering is still an effect of one's own causation, it is one's own desert. It is recognized that one's suffering may come through the instrumentality of another person, but the latter is not credited with any kind of real 'originating agency'. The only kind of personal causation ultimately and properly involved is one's own. 'Each man . . . has prepared the causes of the effects which he now experiences.'[8] 'Each man has . . . several "karmas" . . . yet all quite properly *his, else he would not have found himself subject to their sway.*'[9] What is said here is significant, since the acknowledgement of the inter-relation of events is not permitted to modify the theory of their causation. This is the crucial point at which the Buddhist understanding differs from the view of interdependence set forward in this study. Buddhism speaks of an inter-relation which postulates only one's own causation, or guilt. The hypothesis I would wish to set forward is that genuine interdependence requires the recognition of the interplay of genuinely different personal causes, the recognition of innocence as well as of guilt. It may be tragic that the innocent should suffer, but it is not impossible—on the contrary.

The other point at which the lateral principle has influenced Buddhist thought may be seen in the contrast in the understanding of salvation between the two major schools of Buddhism. The ideal figure of Theravada Buddhism is the Arhant, or self-perfected person. Any 'saviour concept' is meaningless here. This is consonant with the recognition of self-causation as the only type of causation. Salvation is of oneself, by oneself. There is no reference to others, either as creating the conditions which make salvation necessary, or as helping towards the realization of salvation. Nor is any such reference possible, since the individual is and must be completely self-sufficient. Vicariousness is alien to the classic Buddhist concept of salvation. It is precluded by the given framework of reference, which is an exclusively linear model.

By contrast, the chief characteristic of the Boddhisattva of the more developed Mahayana school is compassion, a concern for others. This is not the same as innocent suffering (though one might remind oneself that such an idea is etymologically involved in our words 'sympathy' and 'compassion'). But compassion is an expression of the lateral principle, and the recognition of compassion is not only significant in itself but might well serve as a basis for a wider understanding of vicariousness in general.

A kind of doctrine of vicarious salvation is recognized by a minority, the 'Pure Land' schools of Buddhism, but it is a late development which has been labelled 'clearly anathema to the original Teaching'.[10] In any case, the vicarious salvation of the Pure Land schools is entirely a matter of the transfer of merit, namely, from a Boddhisattva to other men. It involves no recognition of innocent or vicarious *suffering*, which is alien to its concept of vicarious salvation. To offer one's store of merit from good deeds to one's fellow men is the only kind of vicariousness recognized. Without the understanding of suffering as genuinely innocent, one cannot hope to attain to a view of suffering as a burden borne *for* others, namely, vicarious suffering. Any kind of suffering with an altruistic reference has to be precluded. It is not merely that righteous persons *are* rewarded (i.e. acquire merit). It is also understood that righteous persons can *only* be rewarded, i.e. that the righteous *cannot* suffer, which is a rather different proposition. It is not logically impossible to suppose a righteous person to have the capacity both for being rewarded and for undergoing (innocent) suffering. But the possibility of this kind of correlation is unacceptable to the theory we are considering.

To conclude: the idea of karma is an impressive attempt—certainly one of the most developed and systematic—to deal with the consequences of wrongdoing and with the question of suffering. But it would seem in various ways to point beyond itself, towards some implication of interdependence. It is this direction that we shall now pursue. In particular, we shall consider the possibility of the recognition of *innocent* suffering.

The Book of Job is of great importance for the way in which it opens up questions, opens up the possibility of their being asked. It does not in fact go far towards supplying answers, but to criticize it for this is to miss its real emphasis. The Book of Job does not take the questions for granted—as we do, since it is now a commonplace of western thought to assume that there is such a thing as innocent suffering—but rather it portrays the crucial shift of thought that leads from a state of unquestioning to one of urgent inquiry.

A classic and well-known statement of the equation theory of sin and suffering is to be found as the presupposition of the Book of Job. All sin brings suffering to the sinner in its train; all suffering is guilty suffering, i.e. a consequence in the sufferer of his own sin. The first half of this theory, taken by itself, need not have caused anguish to Job. It was quite acceptable as the norm of justice. 'Is not ruin prescribed for the miscreant and calamity for the wrongdoer?'[11] But the second half of the theory is damning, and this is the aspect on which attention is concentrated. Suffering (any and all suffering) is and must be guilty suffering. There is no room for a surplus of suffering, to be interpreted in terms of innocence.

Thus, the question which presents itself to Job is not—straightforwardly—why does he, a righteous man, suffer? Since suffering within the given frame of reference has the connotation of guilty suffering, the question is more explicitly, why is a righteous man—Job's righteousness is established in great detail—treated as a wrongdoer, namely, by the infliction of suffering? Job's chief concern is with his *vindication*, rather than with his release from suffering in itself. The two are linked, of course, but the distinction in emphasis is significant. The first step is to establish that a suffering righteous man is genuinely righteous, and yet, as we have seen, in some theories this step never gets taken. The seemingly righteous has either committed some secret sin, or he is implicated in the guilt of some ancestor; or he may be held to have existed prior to this life and to have committed some wrong in a previous existence. Thus, the 'righteous man' may be wholly or partly righteous in himself and yet personally culpable, as in the latter two alternatives, or else he may not be genuinely righteous at all. This is the 'secret sin' theory, which Job's comforters put forward. At all events, some effort of greater or lesser plausibility is made to maintain the theory of guilty suffering. It is therefore quite a considerable advance actually to reach the belief that there can truly be a suffering righteous person, an innocent sufferer. There is no problem if one clings to some attenuated version of the theory of guilty suffering, but this is at base an evasion of the problem. In the reality of experience it may be claimed that not all suffering is guilty suffering. Some suffering cannot be accounted for in this way, and hence it is problematical. It is problematical precisely because it is innocent and not guilty, and so one must *advance* if one is to attempt to solve the problem and not backtrack by trying to undermine the statement of the issue. This is a perennial temptation to anyone confronted with this problem, since the universal tendency of the human mind is to explain away as much suffering as possible in terms of guilty suffering.

In the Book of Job, unquestioned theory comes into conflict with undeniable experience. Job, who himself accepts the equation theory, as well as the others, is driven to feel that the given facts may not be interpreted by the standard theory. Out of his anguish is born the assertion that not all suffering is guilty suffering, that there is such a thing as innocent suffering. However, although Job leads one away from the equation theory towards the acceptance of the reality of the suffering of the innocent, it does not go far in exploring the significance of this reality. It is established that not all suffering is guilty suffering, but this is basically a qualification to the theory of guilty suffering, rather than a theory of innocent suffering in its own right. It would still tend to assume that the primary meaning of suffering, and its actual meaning in most instances, is that of guilty suffering. The 'surplus' of suffering may be acknowledged, but it is not accounted for. However, it is established that suffering is not intrinsically guilt-bearing, even if a genuine affliction. It does not necessarily imply a condemnation of the person suffering, as the equation theory would require.

Job takes as its premiss the equation theory, which regards all suffering as guilty suffering. It questions this view and rejects it, reaching the conclusion that not all suffering is guilty suffering. It is of particular importance to note that this recognition of innocent suffering is *not* its starting-point, as so many commentators would assume. *We* take the fact of innocent suffering for granted, and we tend to assume that there has been general recognition of this, which the discussion has shown not to be true. It is a very notable achievement to recognize the fact of genuinely *innocent* suffering, and sometimes the step towards this recognition does not get taken. Some views of the world relate sin and suffering only in terms of the equation theory, and this theory closes the door to so many developments. The value of Job is that it reopens all these. It creates possibilities, even if it does not significantly develop them. To repeat, *it does not attempt to answer a question that is already taken for granted.* That is our view and our problem, and to read it into Job is anachronistic. The task of Job is to repudiate an inadequate way of looking at things. It would perhaps not be entirely trite to say that it questions an answer, rather than answers a question. This may seem to render it largely negative and preparatory in scope, but this is not to belittle its significance. It renders a major service by opening up many possibilities, and provides guidelines and safeguards for the way ahead. Theories that follow up what is said by Job may not return to what it rejects, namely, the tendency to explain away in terms of guilty suffering. If in fact they do so, it is probably because they mistakenly consider Job to be on a par with themselves, i.e. to be an attempt to answer a given question—which, as has been argued, is a misleading way of looking at the Book, and confuses its hard-won conclusions with its original premisses. Job prepares the way for discussions of the problem of innocent suffering, but it is not itself such a discussion.

It will be useful for us to bear in mind that the problem of innocent suffering is not one which arises, as it were, *ex nihilo*. We tend to assume that our question is primary, and to forget that it would seem very largely to presuppose some version of the equation theory. It is the rejection of the equation theory, which we see to be a premature and incomplete solution to the interpretation of the phenomenon of suffering, that *raises* the problem as we know it.

Similarly, Job is not theodicy in the commonly understood sense. It is theodicy of its own kind, in that it discusses the justice of God, and hence naturally falls within the definition of theodicy. But our own particular understanding of theodicy is articulated around the problem of innocent suffering, hence any discussion which does not presuppose this particular problem may not be taken as theodicy as we know it.

We are not claiming that at the time of the writing of the Book of Job the equation theory met with general acceptance. In practice, instances of innocent suffering may have been recognized. But the equation theory was prominent as a theoretical formulation, and it required the Book of Job to apply a decisive blow to it—though of course even now lingering traces remain in western thought, so deeply rooted is the tendency to interpret suffering as that of the guilty. However, Job stands as a protest against the scholasticism of the Wisdom Tradition of the Old Testament and against any other system which claims to interpret experience in terms of the equation theory.

## SUFFERING, INNOCENT AND GUILTY

In actual fact, despite the acceptance of the equation theory as premiss, not all affliction is seen by Job as guilt-bearing. Widows, orphans, and the poor are seen as people to be helped[12]—something which, arguably, would not be enjoined if it were seen as subverting the course of justice, rather than as promoting it. This is not to rule out the suggestion that guilty sufferers should in some way be helped, but this is perhaps an idea of a sophistication beyond the scope of the Book of Job. Poverty is at the same time a special case. Parallel to the sin/suffering equation theory, usually referred to as *the* equation theory, one also has the doctrine that righteousness and prosperity are reciprocally linked (righteousness leads to prosperity; prosperity is the reward of righteousness). And yet we have seen that the poor are not spoken of in a derogatory way, as if poverty implied unrighteousness, but as fitting objects of compassion. This suggests the thought that a rigid application of either of these equation theories would be detrimental to ethical obligations, and yet these are important for Job. At this point we discover a marked weakness in the structure of these theories.

The possible significance of the suffering of the righteous is not treated at length. Only one suggestion is offered, that the righteous may suffer in order that their faith may be tested—and this, in order to prove the possibility of disinterested goodness. It is the righteousness/prosperity doctrine that receives a particularly severe blow from the application of the testing theory. Indeed, if it is the testing theory that one considers specifically, one sees that it is far more subversive of the righteousness/prosperity doctrine than of the sin/suffering doctrine. It does itself suggest a qualification to the theory of guilty suffering, but in its direct application it attempts to probe the possibilities of disinterested, unrewarded goodness. If at the same time it shatters the equation theory of sin and suffering, this is but a side-effect of its main purpose! To recapitulate: the two sets of terms subscribed to were the sin/suffering equation and the righteousness/prosperity equation. To replace the first term of the first equation by the first term of the second equation is not merely to alter the first equation but the second as well. Indeed, the treatment of the second equation must take a kind of priority, in that the *testing* theory by definition refers to the testing of righteousness. Innocent suffering is involved by the latter; though this is not to say, conversely, that all innocent suffering is necessarily a testing of righteousness. However, as far as the testing theory is concerned, the real topic under consideration is the possibility of disinterested goodness, not the possibility of innocent suffering as such—though the first makes possible the second, and the two come to be linked.

It would seem that the righteousness/prosperity doctrine is not in practice regarded as so all-embracing as the sin/suffering doctrine. Prosperity should be the hallmark of goodness on this theory, but it is acknowledged that often the wicked also prosper, if temporarily. However, if prosperity need not be tied to one signification, why should suffering be tied in this way? If the one kind of equation theory is subject to this ambivalence, this in turn suggests the possibility of questioning the other equation theory at the same point. The established theory would have assumed that suffering called righteousness into question. The rejection of this theory allows and even asserts that suffering may actually be a way of establishing the reality of righteousness—a paradoxical thought. This also does away with the inconsistency we have just touched on: under the old theory evil was taken to be evil, and even subsequent prosperity—presumed to be temporary—did not alter this estimate. Righteousness, however, was only considered righteous so long as and on condition that it was followed by prosperity. Subsequent suffering led to the revision of the original estimate, as Job's comforters attempted to do. Thus, the genuineness of righteousness might well have been called into question, unfairly, though not the reality of evil.

Job's revision of the criteria for estimating righteousness opens the way for further theories linking the terms 'righteousness' and 'suffering'. For until it is seen that the two terms can be linked in some way, without questioning the reality of either term, it is impossible to advance towards any theories of 'creative' or 'vicarious' suffering, which we would find significant. The Book of Job provides the necessary groundwork on which to base subsequent developments. Job establishes that the righteous can suffer while yet being righteous, and from this one can go on to explore the possible significance of their suffering. This conclusion, based on the testing theory, is to be linked with the other conclusion that is established in the Book of Job: that not all suffering is guilty suffering, that there is such a thing as innocent suffering. The two conclusions are separately reached, but reinforce each other and must be seen together. There is such a thing as innocent suffering, *and* the righteous can suffer. Both points are important, as forming the basis for the understanding of vicariousness.

One should note that the testing theory only forms the background to the Book of Job. One is presented with a drama working simultaneously on two levels of insight: the celestial court accepts the possibility of the testing theory and does not regard it as problematical, but the human actors are unaware of this possibility and remain dominated by the guilt-bearing view. Thus, although innocent suffering and the testing of righteousness are linked in Job, it is interesting to see how there are concurrently two different emphases as a result of these two factors. From the point of view of the man Job himself, the question is one of the suffering of the innocent. He seeks vindication, and the view suggested by the prose conclusion is that his *innocence* is demonstrated, in the established manner. From the point of view of God, however, the question is one of the testing of righteousness or—more specifically—disinterested goodness. This test is satisfactorily accomplished by Job's performance under suffering, and the restoration mentioned by the prose conclusion is irrelevant. Job's righteousness has already been established—his righteousness rather than his innocence. Two questions are simultaneously being asked. They are closely connected, but are not by any means identical, and so there are two different answers to be sought. It is not, as is so often thought, a matter of Job presenting two answers to one question. It is quite simply that each answer belongs to a genuinely different question in the first place.

Job establishes the presence of the problematical in the question of suffering. He does so by rejecting a particularly rigid view of the connection between sin and suffering, which is not—one must insist—the same as rejecting the possibility of guilty suffering altogether. Indeed, guilt is held to call for suffering, and until suffering has come as a consequence things are held to be in an unsatisfactory state. For Job the only kind of suffering that is problematical is innocent suffering. In this way Job does not anticipate a certain interesting trend in present-day thought which would question the idea that the guilty should suffer. If this trend were to be followed through, every kind of suffering would become problematical, not just one sort. One might still speak of a problem of innocent suffering, but one would also have to consider a problem of guilty suffering. Indeed, if it is held *wrong* (in some sense) for the guilty to suffer, then even guilty suffering becomes—paradoxically—a sort of 'innocent' suffering. The whole scheme whereby the theme of guilt predominated and innocence was but a qualification to this, could be totally upturned.

It is interesting that theories of innocent suffering and of guilty suffering have developed along opposite lines. Innocent suffering—after it had been established that there was such a thing—became firstly problematical, because it was not guilty suffering, and subsequently to some extent valuable. Guilty suffering—the occurrence of which one did not doubt—was firstly taken for granted as being of some value, and only now looks like becoming problematical. However, if guilty suffering becomes problematical, this must lead to revision of one's estimate of the problematical nature of innocent suffering—the criterion of which was that it was not guilty suffering, which was an accepted, non-problematical phenomenon. Innocent suffering was found to be problematical just because it was innocent, rather than guilty. Guilty suffering by definition cannot be problematical on the same terms. Is suffering then to be considered problematical on non-moral considerations, or at any rate on some consideration which would no longer find it relevant to distinguish between the suffering of the (morally) innocent and the (morally) guilty? Did the Book of Job not go far enough in its questioning? Certainly guilty suffering is not held problematical by it. Or has modern thought gone too far? It is rapidly losing any sense of the meaning or value of guilty suffering, and thus also risks being unable to assign any value to any kind of suffering. Although its direct impact is on the value of the suffering of the guilty, this might indirectly undermine theories of innocent suffering as well.

What in fact is the theory of guilty suffering proposed by Job? I mean by this Job's assessment of suffering that *is* proven to be guilty, and not Job's qualification of the overall theory of guilty suffering. In other words, the assessment of the (kind of) suffering that is guilty, rather than the assessment of suffering, which is (altogether, on the old theory) guilty. The old theory did, of course, simplify matters. If it was taken as valid, then suffering was quite simply the criterion of guilt, both in a demonstrative sense—'this man's suffering indicates that he is guilty'; and in an instrumental sense—'suffering is the means by which the guilty is treated as he deserves'. By establishing that not all suffering is guilty suffering, one is no longer entitled to speak simplistically of suffering as the criterion of guilt—especially since, in addition to the qualification of the guilty suffering theory, suffering is seen as capable of establishing righteousness, in the 'testing' theory. Thus, suffering may be as much the measure of righteousness as of guilt. The connection between the words 'guilty' and 'suffering' is still seen as proper (occasionally), but no longer as necessary; and in many instances the two terms are not in fact to be connected.

Guilty suffering, in the more restricted sense now established, is seen as disciplinary. This is a useful insight, but it is not developed at length by the Book of Job. The fact of guilty suffering is presupposed, though its application is restricted. The disciplinary theory comments on what is taken for granted, whereas the testing theory is an innovation, particularly important for the support it gives to the establishment of the fact of innocent suffering. The disciplinary theory is descriptive of (only) guilty suffering, while the testing theory is descriptive of (only) innocent suffering. To say that suffering for Job is either disciplinary or testing, without expanding this statement as above, is to be in danger of overlooking Job's hard-won distinction between the two kinds of suffering, and forgetting what a considerable advance in thought this constituted at the time.

It is established that there is a surplus of suffering. Even to call it a surplus, though, implies the primacy of the guilty suffering theory. What can be subsumed to it is considered as being accounted for. What can not be subsumed to it is as it were an 'absurd' quantity, not an explicable remainder. Innocent suffering is not subject to immediate accountability. This is because it is in a significant sense non-consequential. This is not to denote it uncaused, since the immediate causal factors resulting in suffering are ascertainable in a world governed by natural causation. But it is not the consequence of the sufferer's guilt, by definition. Nor, even if the sufferer's character is being tested, is it a consequence of his goodness in a manner comparable to instances where suffering is a consequence of wrongdoing. The only consequence of goodness, in this sense, is taken to be prosperity. And when in the Book of Job this theory is shaken, it is not to replace prosperity by establishing suffering in its position, but to show that prosperity is irrelevant as a consequence (the heavenly court is satisfied with Job's proven goodness before he is restored to prosperity). In this way it is suggested that there is not an inherent connection between righteousness and prosperity, and certainly not a reciprocal one, since even the wicked may prosper for a time.

This would appear to constitute a definite point of difference between the two types of suffering. Guilty suffering is taken to be a consequence of wrongdoing, but even if (innocent) suffering may be capable of proving the quality of goodness, it is not a consequence of it. Thus, too, innocent suffering is not in any way predictable. One may say of guilty suffering where it should come, namely, to a wrongdoer. The wicked may prosper, but this is nevertheless regarded as something ethically incongruous, and thus only reinforces the demand for wickedness to 'meet with its desert'. However, one cannot say where innocent suffering 'should' come. It is a non-predictable phenomenon, inasmuch as it is not a consequence of righteousness, and no act or manifestation of righteousness can justify the statement that suffering *should* follow it.

Guilty suffering may be a predictable phenomenon in the sense just mentioned, but this is not to dictate the circumstances of its realization. Immediate realization certainly cannot be compelled and, if conceivably everyone had to 'pay their own consequences' at once, this would detract from the concept of responsibility rather than enhance it. Instant fulfilment would be as much an inadequate approach as any form of time-dominated equation theory. The time-factor cannot be excluded altogether, but it should be prevented from wrongfully dominating the problem at hand. The quest is for a solution that does not rest on or require any kind of distortion.

# 4
# Dealing with Consequences

It will by now be evident that the model of the 'equation theory' is insufficient for the interpretation of experience. Not all suffering is a consequence of wrongdoing in the person of the wrongdoer, i.e. not all suffering is guilty suffering: there is such a thing as innocent suffering. However, this discovery disposes of only the second half of the equation theory. The first half—that sin leads to suffering for the wrongdoer—has not been affected. It is simply that we can no longer assume as a corollary that *all* suffering is a manifestation of this principle.

The idea that wrongdoing leads to suffering for the wrongdoer is capable of varying interpretation.[1] In particular, is the link between the two an intrinsic one or a matter of external imposition? Punishment or any other measure of individual or social action evidently belongs to the latter category. But does this exhaust the connection between wrongdoing and suffering; and, if not, what is the relation between the two kinds of link? Indeed, it might be asked what need there is for an external link if there is an intrinsic one.

As a preliminary to answering these questions we shall describe some of the ways in which the link has hitherto been interpreted, in terms of three broad categories. The first is the stage at which the consequences of wrongdoing are proliferated. At the second stage consequences are checked and not furthered. Some action may be taken against the wrongdoer, but such an action stands by itself and is not the first of a further series of actions. But no attempt is made to do more than merely check consequences. At the third stage, however, the consequences of wrongdoing are not only checked but transformed. These three categories will be subject to a varying moral assessment. They are in effect advancing stages, the one giving place to the other, and the further advanced being considered morally preferable to the former. In practical terms, of course, the advance from stage to stage is neither smoothly clear-cut nor irrevocable, e.g. one might not wish for lapses into revenge, but it is not impossible for this to happen. However, this model of the three stages will provide some kind of theoretical framework for our discussion, and is intended to shed light on some of the principles or mechanisms involved in dealing with the consequences of wrongdoing.

The first stage proliferates or escalates the consequences of wrongdoing, in a continuing chain of actions and counter-actions. It prolongs consequences or, it might be said, lets them run to exhaustion. This kind of approach readily lends itself to formulation in terms of an equation theory, with all its concomitant difficulties of dominance by the time-factor. We have already seen how the system of karma requires consequences to run until exhaustion, and how the concept of reincarnation is introduced to guarantee this; and how, in addition, it is postulated that all suffering must exemplify this outworking of consequences. However, the first stage need not be exemplified only by the equation theory. The idea of nemesis is very similar in some ways to that of karma, but differs significantly in that, although itself descriptive of guilty suffering, it is not tied to an assertion that all suffering is guilty suffering. Nemesis does not attempt to account for all experience in the way that karma does. It bases itself on the first half of the equation theory alone, namely, that sin leads to suffering for the wrongdoer, and describes this in terms of the proliferation of consequences.

Nemesis could theoretically be worked out within the lifetime of a single individual. Usually, however, it goes on to involve several successive generations. In addition, although stemming from one particular act, in the first generation, it may be reinforced by subsequent acts of other persons, though these are considered as in some way subordinate to the first and most significant act. One sees how the time-factor affects the presentation of this theory. Consequences must be worked out; and, although members of subsequent generations are not regarded as reincarnations of the first generation, they are required to shoulder the responsibility that most strictly belongs to the first person involved. There is no equation of identity here, but it may well be considered that the underlying notion of responsibility is questionable. It would be permissible to say that all—whether innocent or guilty—share in the general consequences of a given act of wrongdoing, but it is improper to interpret this in terms of

## DEALING WITH CONSEQUENCES

punishment, which refers to the guilty party alone. If the first act of wrongdoing is reinforced by subsequent acts, then a sharing of guilt may be postulated. But a balance needs to be preserved. When, as is usual with the nemesis pattern, the subsequent acts are seen primarily as the outworking of the first act, and are subordinated to it, it is difficult to assign an equivalent proportion of responsibility to the subsequent acts. By what right does one say that a person of the second generation is responsible not merely for his own action, but—by this very deed—for the action of the original wrongdoer in the first generation? (Unless one postulates identity of the two actors, by the device of reincarnation—which we have taken to be an unacceptable solution.) The pattern is further complicated if, as in the Oresteia, subsequent actions are intended as the outworking of justice for the antecedent actions, and yet are themselves to be considered criminal. Killing is avenged by killing, and itself demands further action to be taken on its own account. This is the appalling dilemma of the classical pattern of nemesis, where to meet the claims of justice is to set up yet a further demand for justice. However, this particular complication is not essential to the nemesis pattern, even though a striking feature of some of its best-known examples. It is possible for a succession of calamities to be interpreted as nemesis following on some given original act—that is, these calamitous happenings may be interpreted solely in terms of the original act, and need not individually call for further satisfaction.

The nemesis pattern may be found in various forms. The best-known, that of Greek tragedy, has already been mentioned, and indeed it is the Greek word *nemesis* that has passed into our vocabulary. The Judaeo-Christian tradition also contains this kind of idea. Acts may be said to affect people 'unto the third and fourth generation'. However, this form of the collective idea lent itself to abuse, and the protest of Ezekiel is well-known. The popular proverb, 'The fathers have eaten sour grapes, and the children's teeth are set on edge'[2] is denounced in some detail as pernicious. Instead, it is asserted that 'It is the soul that sins, and no other, that shall die; a son shall not share a father's guilt, nor a father his son's. The righteous man shall reap the fruit of his own righteousness, and the wicked man the fruit of his own wickedness.'[3] This is not to preclude any notion of corporate solidarity, but serves as a protest against abuses of the collective idea.

Linear responsibility is asserted—not to the exclusion of lateral responsibility, but against the mistaken idea that the lateral is the only form of responsibility, which is to render assignation of responsibility quite chaotic. If people are not responsible for their own actions, on what basis is it possible to assert that they are in any sense responsible for those of other people? In the absence of linear responsibility it seems improbable that one may be considered responsible at all.

Another theological idea which is traditionally expressed in terms of a nemesis pattern is that of original sin. Adam sinned, and all are implicated in the consequences of his act. St Paul says of this: 'It was through one man that sin entered the world, and through sin death, and thus death pervaded the whole human race, inasmuch as all men have sinned.'[4] The wording here is vital. 'Inasmuch as all men have sinned' is a fair rendering of the Greek *eph'ho pantes hemarton*. However, *eph'ho* was rendered into Latin as *in quo*, and thus the entire meaning was altered: 'Since *in* Adam all men sinned.' Augustine and the mainstream of exegesis followed this path for many centuries. In this seemingly small point of language lies all the difference between two widely contrasting views of collective responsibility. Is guilt imputed to all men '*in* Adam', irrespective of their own character; or is there an actual sharing of guilt, *inasmuch as* all men have sinned?

The nemesis pattern is prone to meet with difficulties over the allocation of responsibility, perhaps because it is mistakenly assumed that to share in the consequences of wrongdoing is and must be interpreted as some form of punishment, and that anyone thus affected must therefore be guilty. This is not the case. Indeed, the first person affected by wrongdoing is the wrongdoer's victim, and then perhaps those connected with the victim, who are all innocent parties sharing in the consequences of the wrongdoer's act. We would not claim that these are being punished, or the wrongdoer—mistakenly so-called—would really be the executor of justice. Likewise, we are not automatically entitled to assume that any other persons, e.g. the wrongdoer's descendants, are necessarily *punished* for the wrongdoer's act. The first step is to establish guilt, not to assert that any sharing in the consequences of wrongdoing of itself implies guilt, which would be to make the kind of mistake committed by the equation theory. It would seem that the nemesis pattern is prone to describe everything in terms of punishment when it might often be more fair to speak of the more general sharing of the consequences of wrongdoing by persons not liable to punishment. It is important to attempt as much accuracy as is possible in the use of the collective idea, for confusion here is both untruth and injustice.

Similarly with vendetta which, as a system of unceasing retaliation, permits of treating the innocent as the guilty when 'justice is done' on others besides the wrongdoer. Again, the notion of collective responsibility involved is of dubious propriety. It differs from the scheme of nemesis, however, through comprising human actions alone for its outworking and not including natural calamities. And in a sense one might speak of vendetta as a 'demythologized' form of nemesis, which is itself a less rigorous version of the first half of the full-scale metaphysical system of karma.

The second stage deals with consequences by checking them. The contrast with the first stage is marked by the transition from vendetta to the *lex talionis*. This marks an advance in thought which is scarcely remembered now that the *lex talionis* idea has itself been advanced on. Christ said, 'You have learned that they were told, "Eye for eye, tooth for tooth." But what I tell you is this: Do not set yourself against the man who wrongs you.'[5] This, however, is an expression of the transition from the second stage to the third stage, and it was once a marked achievement to have reached the second stage. The idea of *only* a tooth for a tooth took the place of the idea that it was fitting to knock out every tooth a man had in return for one tooth knocked out.

The *lex talionis* thus marks a kind of quantitative difference, which at the same time represents a step forward in ethical thought. The other notable characteristic of the *lex talionis* is the importance it attaches to similarity—similarity between the act of wrongdoing and the treatment meted out to the wrongdoer. 'Eye for eye, tooth for tooth' was once taken literally, and physical injury met with similar mutilation. Precision was of course difficult to achieve at times. (What is the right treatment for a man who knocks out one eye, when it is the only seeing eye of his victim? What is to be done about a childless man who cripples his neighbour's son? These and many other examples bedevilled the working of the *lex talionis*.) And, in course of time, the strict form of the *lex talionis* was commuted in favour of money payment or other forms of treatment. But the advance on the first stage was preserved, and thus the lasting achievement of the *lex talionis* was that it rendered vendetta and the like obsolete.

However, the second stage has to be contrasted with the stage that follows it as well as with the stage which it supersedes. The *lex talionis* illustrates the first part of the transition, from the proliferation to the checking of consequences. The contrast with the third stage is best marked by the idea of deterrence: consequences are checked, but are no more than checked.

It is important to remember that we are considering the deterrence of the wrongdoer, i.e. of one who has already committed wrong and thus of one who has—in the given instance of wrongdoing—*not* been deterred. To be more precise, we should speak of subsequent deterrence—the future deterrence of one who has not previously been deterred. It is vital to spell this out, since the lack of this has led to considerable confusion. If punishment is for deterrence, then why—it is sometimes asked—should not the innocent be punished, in order to deter them? Whether or not expressed in so many words, this idea does tend to lurk in current discussion, and results from an inability to distinguish between primary and secondary deterrence. One may certainly attempt to deter non-wrongdoers from committing wrong, but this primary deterrence is the task of crime prevention, not of punishment. Punishment may include deterrence, but by definition it applies to the wrongdoer—one who has already committed wrong, who has not been deterred from so doing—and hence it should be spoken of as subsequent or secondary deterrence. The question asked about 'punishing' the innocent in order to deter them is rendered nonsensical if its implications are spelled out, i.e. 'If punishment is for deterring those who have not previously been deterred from committing crime, why should not non-criminals—who have previously been deterred—be punished?' There is no sense in this question, though it is none other than the question often asked, in more ambiguous language, in current discussion. Refusal to distinguish between primary and secondary deterrence is again a misuse of the corporate idea, an improper allocation of responsibility.

The person who has committed wrong is to be deterred from committing further wrong. The fact that deterrence implies some kind of change of heart indicates that in practice it will be difficult always to separate deterrence from reformation. However, it is possible for a person to be merely deterred, and it is important to be able to draw the theoretical distinction between deterrence and reformation. The third stage is that of the transformation of the consequences that wrongdoing has for the wrongdoer. This involves a complete change of heart on the part of the wrongdoer—his reformation or return to the good.

It will be evident that the three stages must mark different understandings of the importance of the disposition of the wrongdoer. Concern for the wrongdoer's moral disposition is only genuinely established at the second stage. At the first stage this was hardly possible, thanks to the widespread allocation (misallocation) of responsibility. *To focus on the wrongdoer alone is the essential prerequisite of a concern with the moral effect of punishment*, and hence it is only at this point—unburdened by improper concepts of corporate responsibility—that we begin to develop this concern properly. The three stages represent a kind of process of increasing interiorization, until by the third stage the effect on the wrongdoer's personality becomes of paramount importance. This is not, it should be noted, a movement away from infliction, since all three stages retain this—understood not as anything necessarily harsh but simply as something imposed on the wrongdoer by another party. The progression is away from a stage where infliction may be understood as an end in itself; towards the understanding of infliction as an instrument for rendering the inner disposition accessible.

It may be asserted that almost any theory of punishment currently accepted does set a premium on the wrongdoer's disposition, even if it does not state this in so many words, simply on a piece of negative evidence: any method of dealing with an offender which falls short of total and permanent physical incapacitation—the only guaranteed way of ensuring no further trouble—must by this very fact be allowing some scope for the offender's disposition. More positively, there is usually some concern for this, though varying from theory to theory. The wrongdoer's state of mind, which was such as to allow him to do wrong in the first place, is to be changed, whether partially modified or fully transformed. It is, of course, difficult to assess this accurately in practice. However, this does not justify the substitution of some lesser and less desirable goal which would belittle the importance of these factors of personality. The difficulty of measurement may be the perennial problem of the practice of punishment, but one cannot dispose of the problem by giving up the attempt at assessment altogether—unless one wishes to give up any form of dealing with the offender, which is quite another matter and in effect implies a willingness to let the situation remain unmodified.

Wrongdoing has moral consequences for the wrongdoer. Punishment finds its place when it is held desirable to forestall one type of consequence, i.e. continuation in hardness of heart, and to promote another type of consequence, i.e. returning to goodness. Neither the forestalling of the one (deterrence) nor the promoting of the other (reformation) is something that generally happens automatically. In some instances this may happen spontaneously, and the wrongdoer's disposition may be radically altered without the aid of something from outside of him. But by and large this is not true, and the testimony of human experience is that some aid is needed. Thus, there are two propositions. First, and without qualification, that it is considered desirable for further wrongdoing to be forestalled and for a return to goodness and good behaviour to be promoted. This is the acceptance of the priority of goodness, and the need to tackle wrong, that is presupposed by all theories of punishment. Second, that some instrument seems to be needed for this change, with the qualification that this is not always necessary, but would seem to be generally required. Thus, punishment may be applied as an instrument for dealing with the consequences of wrongdoing in the person of the wrongdoer.

Hardness of heart or moral deterioration may follow on wrongdoing if not checked and forestalled—usually by the agency of punishment, acting as a deterrent agent. Alternatively, penitence and reformation may be promoted—again, normally not without the agency of punishment. It should be clear that these consequences of wrongdoing are distinct from punishment. They are essentially independent of it, though they may be linked to it in practice, in the instrumental relationship described. It is of some importance to be able in this way to distinguish punishment from the consequences of wrongdoing. Punishment is not only instrumental in relation to these particular consequences, but actually derives its meaning in relation to them *and not otherwise*. The current loss of bearings in criminological thought may well be due to focusing too exclusively on punishment by itself, and so it becomes necessary to insist that punishment has no meaning apart from the consideration of wrongdoing and its consequences.

It is further evident from all this that the position of punishment is *intermediate*. It is neither an end in itself, as was mistakenly supposed by traditional retributivism. Nor is punishment its own starting-point, as tends to be supposed at the present time, particularly by those of utilitarian views. Both positions are mistaken, in that each is quite literally one-sided, taking in isolation either the first two terms or the last two terms of what is properly a series of three terms.

This threefold sequence is as follows:

WRONGDOING—PUNISHMENT—CONSEQUENCES

Wrongdoing is and must be the first term of the series. Punishment is subsequent to wrongdoing, but also it is something instrumental, and hence one looks beyond it to see what is effected by its instrumentality. Neither end of the sequence may be omitted without making nonsense of the rest of it.

The *only* term in the series which could, without illogicality, be dropped is in fact that of punishment—the one term which has not hitherto been omitted by either school of thought. It is quite possible to speak of

WRONGDOING—CONSEQUENCES

and by doing this one emphasizes the subordinate position of punishment. Punishment is instrumental, a 'transforming agent'. Hence it may be reintroduced into the series in these terms:

WRONGDOING—TRANSFORMING AGENT—
TRANSFORMED CONSEQUENCES

Although punishment must take the intermediate position in the series, it is something extraneous, introduced to modify the final term of the series. Wrongdoing does not lead on to punishment in the same sense that it leads on to hardness of heart. Rather, punishment is interposed between these two, in order to prevent the latter. Hence also the final term of the series is not something fixed. There are several possibilities, and the task of punishment is to influence which of these is to be realized. Basically, the final term may be one of untransformed consequences, or hardness of heart; or transformed consequences —partially transformed in the case of mere deterrence, or fully transformed in the case of reformation. Hence the series may be expressed like this:

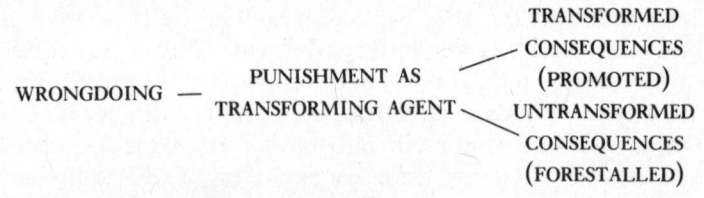

```
                                       TRANSFORMED
                                       CONSEQUENCES
                    PUNISHMENT AS      (PROMOTED)
WRONGDOING  —   TRANSFORMING AGENT
                                       UNTRANSFORMED
                                       CONSEQUENCES
                                       (FORESTALLED)
```

It can be seen from this that it is incorrect to ask whether punishment is either on account of a past offence or for the sake of future good. There is no question of 'either-or', since our analysis of the position of punishment has shown that it is clearly both things. Punishment is both subsequent to wrongdoing, and anticipatory of the final outworking of the consequences of wrongdoing. It is not so much that punishment has a retrospective reference, but that wrongdoing has a prospective reference, and wrongdoing precedes punishment and is its only justification (if there has been no wrongdoing, there can be no call for an agent to deal with the consequences of wrongdoing, i.e. punishment). There is no need for the traditional dichotomy between retrospective and prospective views of punishment, between retributive and utilitarian. It is a false dichotomy, presumably occasioned by a neglect to bear in mind the true position of punishment. It is the consequences of *wrongdoing* that are to be considered, not the consequences of *punishment*. One ought only to speak of 'the consequences of punishment' if one explicitly recognizes that this means 'the modified consequences of wrongdoing'—that and nothing else. At the same time this would clear the air of any latent tendencies to suggest that punishment of the innocent might for some reason be a proper exercise. This would be to neglect the first term of the series—wrongdoing—and to forget that punishment has meaning *only* in relation to wrongdoing and its consequences.

Traditional retributive views often lost sight of the ultimate outcome to which punishment is properly subordinate. It is not that they were wrong in holding that wrongdoing should 'lead on' to punishment, but that they did not go far enough. In emphasizing a part of the truth—a valid and important part—they tended to lose sight of the whole truth. *Why* is it that wrongdoing leads on to punishment? The answer should be: out of a concern for the consequences of wrongdoing, and hence one will naturally look beyond punishment as well, to see what is finally effected by it.

Utilitarianism gathered much of its force in reaction to the one-sidedness of retributivism, in the wish to stress what had been left neglected, namely the effect that punishment has on the consequences of wrongdoing. Unfortunately, it has tended to become one-sided in its turn. Symptomatic of this is its tendency to speak without qualification of the consequences of *punishment*, as if punishment were its own starting-point and did not presuppose wrongdoing and the consequences of wrongdoing. Punishment is not and cannot be anything like a merely forward-looking social hygiene. That is crime prevention; and we have already seen that it is a dangerous mistake to confuse punishment or secondary deterrence with crime prevention or primary deterrence. The fact that wrongdoers are punished and deterred from further wrongdoing does of course support the overall system of crime prevention and primary deterrence, but the two are to be carefully distinguished. Utilitarian thought has in fact generally maintained fairly stringent conditions for the application of punishment—when (after wrongdoing) and on whom (the wrongdoer). Are these, however, a necessary part of utilitarian thought? One suspects that the attempt to correct retributivism could easily go too far, though we have demonstrated that the attempt to deny punishment any kind of retrospective reference is in effect to destroy its meaning altogether. Deterrence and reformation of the wrongdoer *are* aims of punishment—deterrence and reformation *of the wrongdoer*. (It is too easy to read this statement without stressing these all-important words.) The very word 'reformation' should require one to keep in mind the reference to past wrongdoing—otherwise what is there that needs reforming? Reformation speaks of the future, certainly, but only in terms of the transformation of the past. Again, the utilitarian may require punishment to be justified by its effects. This is fair enough, if it is not forgotten that it is *punishment* that is to be thus justified. There is no difficulty about this if it is realized that punishment is an instrument for dealing with the consequences of wrongdoing in the person of the wrongdoer. When punishment is spoken of in these terms, the concern for past and future alike becomes evident.

We have already seen, though, that the future is not something assured. However useful punishment may be as a transforming agent, it is not infallible and there is no guarantee of obtaining certain results. The wrongdoer is free not to undergo a change of heart, or his attitude may only be partially modified. There is no determinism in all this, and one must always remember that the final term of the series is not fixed. Punishment may be the proper means of attempting a change, but neither it nor anything else can force the issue. It may promote, but cannot compel. Utilitarian theory in particular would do well to bear this in mind. To speak of punishing or 'treating' an offender in order to reform him—for his own good and that of society, of course—can be dangerously ambiguous. One may be entitled to make the attempt to reform an offender, but it is quite another thing to insist on reformation, so that an offender may not be released unless and until his reform is guaranteed—presumably even if this were to take the rest of his life. In this way, what may originally have been a genuinely benevolent concern may turn into a deterministic tyranny. Hence we must conclude on a note of caution.

# 5
# The Symbolic Theory of Punishment

To develop the ideas just outlined we shall consider in detail one specific theory of punishment. Our discussion will be based on part two of Sir Walter Moberly's book *The Ethics of Punishment*. The work as a whole considers the philosophy and history of punishment, and is both a survey of other people's thought and an exposition of Sir Walter's own ideas. This very comprehensiveness and combination of purposes has unfortunately resulted in insufficient attention being focused on the most original contribution of the whole study: Sir Walter's thoughts on punishment as symbol, hence the designation 'the symbolic theory' of punishment.

The symbolic theory is a new approach to the understanding of punishment, but at the same time it arises out of the consideration of two widespread and persistent ideas: that punishment 'serves one right', and that with punishment one finds associated a deep craving to undo. Discussion of these takes up the first two chapters of Sir Walter's 'attempt to dig a little deeper'. The result of the discussion is a seeming impasse: the conclusion is reached that 'we cannot *rightly* punish to give "due" and cannot *reasonably* punish in order to undo'.[1] The dilemma is resolved by viewing punishment in terms of symbolism. A three-part discussion ensues, under the general title of 'The sign and the thing signified'. Punishment is spoken of as being a symbol; some more general comments on the uses of symbolism follow; and in conclusion the concept of symbolism is specifically linked to the understanding of the ethical element in punishment. This symbolic theory marks an advance on previous ideas, and at the same time suggests a basis for further discussion; much is hinted at, and needs underlining or further expansion. But first, let us follow the argument as it develops.

The question of desert, its meaning and moral value, is the first point to be tackled,[2] and the discussion takes into account both good and ill desert. People expect voluntary actions to have congruous consequences for the agent—this is a common ethical presupposition, applicable to good and bad actions alike. However, to what extent does good desert provide a satisfactory and genuine parallel for ill desert? To repay good with good is proper and praiseworthy; to repay ill with ill may be natural, but it is the refusal to do this which is considered laudable. To be specific, one finds in the question of ill desert a conflict of principles such as does not arise as regards good desert. The conflict is that to hurt in return for hurt, on the principle of congruity of consequences, clashes with the principle of goodwill. Is it morally justifiable to pay back bad behaviour in kind? This is the major difficulty. A minor difficulty is also suggested: that while a right to a boon or favour may make sense, a right to a bane or ill seems illogical.

More profoundly, what does this kind of approach to 'desert' presuppose about the concepts of reward and punishment? Is it proper to regard happiness as something distinct from goodness, and misery as something separate from wrong? And, as a corollary to this, ought one to consider that happiness and misery can be conferred or withheld by human decision? At a certain level one may think along these lines. But these ideas have only a limited validity and, the more deeply one is prepared to consider them, the less true they are as satisfactory statements of moral experience. Much in the concepts of reward and punishment requires to be outgrown. One may begin by speaking of happiness as the reward of goodness; later, with Spinoza, one may say that happiness is not the reward of goodness, but goodness itself.[3]

> In this view, vice may be said to be its own punishment, just as virtue is its own reward. But in this context 'reward' and 'punishment' are inexact terms and are only used as metaphors.[4]

It is pointed out that, since happiness and unhappiness are states of mind, they cannot be conferred *directly*. One may, in certain instances, award or withhold things conducive to these states, but nevertheless these states are not necessarily dependent on such actions. The main point being made here is that ultimately happiness and misery are not (a) properly calculable; or (b) capable of being conferred or withheld by personal decision. Bearing this in mind, one sees that when 'goods' and 'evils' are conferred these are of a secondary order:

Perhaps the difference between these two 'orders' of evil—and its relevance—can be illustrated by the contrast in common speech between 'de-grade' (with a hyphen) and 'degrade' (without a hyphen). The first is a secondary evil; the second is a primary evil. The first is a conceivable form of legitimate punishment, the second is not. No human authority *can* inflict a primary evil and only a devil would want to do so; it could not if it would and, most certainly, it should not if it could.[5]

Thus one must conclude that

> ... the notion of giving a man his 'due', of making the quality of his faring correspond to the quality of his doing, seems to suffer from a common defect. It is concerned with bestowing 'goods' or 'evils' only of a secondary order. It only commands moral approval (as indeed it only makes sense) at relatively crude and immature levels of moral development.[6]

What, in any case, is it to *deserve*? This is a prior question and draws us into the consideration of motivation. The moral assessment of what a man does derives much from his actual intention. And yet, not only are motives particularly important, they are also of great difficulty to appraise accurately, as anyone faced with the administration of justice realizes only too well. The idea of ill desert may be affirmed from the depths of one's own experience, through self-knowledge and the awareness of a personal sense of guilt. However, even if the concept of desert is a valid one, it does not constitute the highest level of our moral scale: the precise adjustment of claim and counter-claim may be transcended in love.

Retribution may, however, be affirmed in terms of the intrinsic outworking of wrong. The truest—and most congruous—retribution of wickedness is to lead a wicked life and become a wicked person. One cannot hurt others without, in this sense, hurting oneself.

> The most certain and the most terrible retribution of our wrongdoing will then be nothing that is done *to* us, but simply what we ourselves shall have *become* ... The sinner, hardened in impenitence, is not sentenced to death, he commits slow suicide.[7]

Thus the imprint on one's character of wrongdoing is its real retribution. Wrongdoing may bring other consequences, less closely related to itself, according to circumstances and convention; but it must in any case bring moral deterioration. And, although one act of wrongdoing may not completely ruin a character, it does take one a step along this path, and subsequent acts may reinforce this trend. *This* is retribution—not the kind of desert that can be given or withheld; and hence, in effect, *not a pattern for punishment*, which is deliberate social action.

> ... we are now treating of a retribution which nobody inflicts and nobody can avert, since it is inseparable from the act of which it is the retribution.[8]

One cannot inflict this kind of retribution, nor should one even desire it, since such suffering incurred by the wrongdoer is of the same order as the wrong which incurred it.

In short, we cannot impose such retribution even if we would, and we should not even if we could. Such automatic retribution then is no possible basis or model for punishing but only a background against which the choice, to punish or not to punish, has to be made.[9]

To revert to the parallel between good and ill desert, it must be noted that in practice we react quite differently to good behaviour and bad behaviour. Good behaviour is encouraged and confirmed—that is simple enough. Bad behaviour is a more complex matter. Our response is not to confirm it—confirmation is a matter of intrinsic outworking, as we have just shown—but to take steps to counteract it. Sir Walter finds the analogy of medical treatment particularly helpful. '(One) seeks to counter-work the natural process of decay and emphatically not to consummate it.'[10] This, however, has brought our discussion of desert to the point where it must of necessity give way to consideration of a second important idea—the desire to undo or annul. As Sir Walter puts it:

> ... to follow up this clue would be to enter a new world of ideas. The principle of continuity may explain the proper response to good conduct. But to deal rightly with evil behaviour, our own or other people's, we must invoke the very

opposite principle; not co-operation but active resistance, not continuance and extension but reversal.[11]

Discussion of the 'craving to undo' forms the second stage of the argument.[12] Alike, popular thought and philosophy tenaciously hold to this desire for annulment, and they link it with the demand for punishment. Two main questions arise from this, and are considered by Sir Walter: the general question 'At any deep level, is not the whole notion of annulment a vain delusion?' and, more specifically, 'Can punishment annul?'

The thought of undoing is readily open to misunderstanding, or undoing may even seem to be inconceivable. In some instances of wrongdoing restitution may be possible or, in other cases, compensation may be made. But these alternatives do not by any means cover all cases of wrongdoing. And, even when they do apply, to what extent are they satisfactory means of annulling what has happened? Such 'annulment' may be considered merely ersatz.

Two aspects of the consequences of wrongdoing are singled out for attention: the moral degradation of the wrongdoer himself, and the social harm, envisaged 'not so much as the suffering caused to others . . . as the lowering of the moral tone'.[13] To wish to alter these is not futile. A clear distinction can and should be drawn between the different effects of wrongdoing. Some material damage can be made up for. Some quite factually cannot be. Moral effects, however, are potentially more mutable than material ones. They are no less serious, indeed even more so; but they have the capacity for a more radical transformation than material effects, which have to be met from, and are subject to, all the limitations of material resources. The original act of damage or pain may or may not be capable of some kind of restoration, but the moral effects it occasioned may be changed. The given act of wrongdoing has made some difference, but to what extent need it continue to do so?

As mere chronology the past is irrevocable, but as still operative, it can be reversed.[14]

One is not attempting to rewrite history as such. What has been has been, and this remains a fact. But is the given fact in addition to exercise a decisive influence on the subsequent course of history? One may not undo the act in itself, but its consequences may be checked and changed. One does not undo altogether (the word asserts too much), but the continuation of what has happened is open to modification:

> The wrong once done still characterizes both a repentant and an unrepentant wrongdoer; but it characterizes them differently. In this sense, so long as there is any place left for repentance, it is possible at least to modify my past, if not to undo it ... The past cannot literally be undone; but men may so react to it in retrospect that its original significance is reversed.[15]

What is the part of punishment in all this? This brings us to the second question raised—can punishment annul?

Many theorists, as Sir Walter points out, have attempted to speak of punishment in some such terms as annulling or negating crime. But to what extent is this idea valid? In many instances there is, at most, only a rough equivalence between crime and punishment. There is also a more serious objection:

> ... that which makes nonsense of the theory of equivalence is the fatal disparity between any possible medium of punishment and the true wrongdoing. The one is external and material, the other is internal and spiritual.[16]

In practice people tend to forget this disparity, and hence misuse the 'undoing' theory by stating it too absolutely, as if there were only one 'order' to be affected and not two:

> Evil is to be suppressed, but what lies in our power is only some material embodiment of evil, and we so easily slip into the belief that, by suppressing that, we have suppressed the evil. But will, whether good or evil, is not so easily scotched. It is only to a materialist that the gallows can appear a final solution.[17]

We have now considered both the concept of desert and the desire to undo, and the conclusion of the discussion is stated as an apparent impasse:

> ... you cannot *rightly* punish in order to give a man his due when what is due to him is utter and irretrievable moral ruin; your purpose is not attainable by any conceivable punishment and, even if it were attainable, it would be devilish. Again, you

## THE SYMBOLIC THEORY OF PUNISHMENT

cannot *reasonably* punish in order to 'undo' the evil deed on account of which you punish; if punishment could really undo wrong, that would be its strongest possible justification, but it cannot.[18]

However, despite this stated difficulty, which rests on the disparity between the material and the moral, we do not have to give up the attempt to make sense of punishment. Sir Walter sees that a theory of punishment must take this statement of two divergent possibilities into account—but it may do so by reflecting them and attempting to influence them:

> Punishment never *is* itself the intrinsic retribution of wrong; (and) it never can itself undo wrong. Yet, in some sense, it may *represent* both consummation and annulment; and, from that representation, it may derive its moral significance. It is the nature of this twofold representation that we must now explore.[19]

For Sir Walter it was the account of the Dreyfus trial, read in 1895 when he was a boy of thirteen, which provided a powerful impetus to his thought:

> ... I believe that, in this special and highly artificial mode of punishment [viz. the military degradation] may be found a clue to understanding the ethical element in all punishment. So far as punishments aim at anything more than bare deterrence, *they point beyond themselves to something more profound which they symbolize*, and it is in the light of this symbolic reference that their moral quality can be discerned.[20]

On the principle of continuation, wrongdoing sooner or later will meet with natural consequences, namely, the intrinsic outworking of wrongdoing. It is desirable that people should not be shielded from the consequences of their actions. On the other hand, should they be allowed to suffer their full impact, when this full impact would be utterly disastrous? The point is well illustrated in the case of children, who must be educated for responsibility, but kept from inadvertent self-destruction. Something should be substituted for the impact of natural physical consequences which will impress those consequences on the mind of the child, who will thus learn from his situation but not at an unacceptably high price. This applies all the more to natural moral consequences, which are moral deterioration and a diminished capacity for human fellowship. This intrinsic retribution of wrongdoing is of the same dire order of evil as its originating act, and hence people will wish to save the wrongdoer from actually experiencing it. At the same time the wrongdoer must learn to appreciate the consequences of his action. Herein lies the function of punishment, which Sir Walter speaks of as 'some deliberately and artificially contrived pain or humiliation which takes an overt form'.[21] Punishment involves the infliction of some *secondary* evil. It is to be carefully distinguished both from primary evil—the moral evil which is the true desert of wrongdoing—and from the 'undoing' of this primary evil:

> Obviously such a penalty is not itself an automatic consequence of wrongdoing—like the moral deterioration of the wrongdoer; nor, on the other hand, is it the morally requisite counter-stroke of good men and true against evil wherever they confront it, for such reaction and inflicted penalty are never simply identical and the counter-working may not be accompanied by any inflicted penalty at all. But, *though identical with neither, it derives all its moral quality from its relation to both.*[22]

What we must constantly bear in mind is that:

> Beneath all that is arbitrary or conventional, there remains an intrinsically congruous retribution of wrongdoing; and this is simply to continue in evil. But such retribution is no inflicted punishment; it is something of another order and a more deadly character.[23]

Both these ideas, of the continuation in evil and of its counter-working, must be borne in mind and interpreted in terms of moral experience. We should understand that neither of these is punishment as such, and hence it becomes of particular importance to be able to distinguish between what punishment *is* and what it *signifies*. What any given instance of punishment *is* may be largely a matter of convention:

> It is neither a necessary natural consequence of the crime nor does it directly 'undo'. But it suggests, and is widely if subconsciously felt to suggest, both consummation and annulment. And its moral quality lies just in this symbolic reference.[24]

Punishment signifies more than is *prima facie* apparent, but nevertheless it is not to be identified with its referents. Sir Walter suggests that the inability to draw these distinctions has led to the deficiencies of both the utilitarian and the retributive schools of thought. To ignore the symbolic aspect of punishment—the fact that it is intended to signify something beyond itself—would be the mistake of the utilitarian. To confuse the sign with the thing signified would be the mistake of the retributionist.

All this does of course presuppose the priority of the good, as is the common assumption of criminological thought. Desert and undoing alike make sense only in such a context, and the demand for them arises when wrong is committed. They are the background to punishment. Punishment, which presupposes them, adds as it were a ritual element by which it signifies them. 'It gives expression and calls attention to *a situation which is anyhow real, whether thus expressed or not.*'[25]

> ... it is designed to symbolize, and it is felt to symbolize, the twofold retribution inherent in the situation, the moral deterioration which is automatic, and the counter-stroke which is obligatory.[26]

There are two orders of evil: the first order of moral evil, and the second order of physical evil. Punishment involves the infliction of an evil and in this it bears a likeness to wrongdoing, which is also an evil. But (*nota bene*) these are evils of different orders. It could never be right to wish to inflict an evil of the first order, and in any case it is beyond human ability to do so; but evils of the second order can be inflicted, and in certain circumstances it may be right to do so. It may sometimes be right to hurt.

Punishment as something external is intended to mirror the inward reality of the situation, and—more than merely depict it—to effect some change in it. The process of moral deterioration which is the reality of retribution may be quite gradual, perhaps even imperceptible. By punishment it is hoped to arrest this process. In this way punishment functions as a kind of danger signal in the moral sphere, comparable to the function of physical pain in the biological sphere. Moral ruin is foreshadowed precisely in order that it may *not* be achieved. The secondary evil of punishment typifies the primary evil of moral and spiritual deterioration and, by foreshadowing it, seeks to forestall it. It is as it were 'an outward and visible sign of an inner and spiritual reality'; an efficacious sign, or 'a kind of inverted sacrament'.[27]

> Its object is, not to effect or to ratify that which it images, but to bring it to naught. So far as the evil has already been accomplished, it is to be 'undone'; so far as it has not yet been accomplished, it is to be for ever prevented.[28]

We must remember, however, that it would be inaccurate to speak of punishment as referring to deterioration alone. Its symbolism is twofold. It images the deterioration implicit in the concept of desert; and it images the counterworking implicit in the desire to undo. It takes into account the *two* drives which have been the perennial mainstay of the discussion of punishment. Instead of choosing between them, as many have done ('punishment must be *either* a matter of desert *or* a matter of undoing'), Sir Walter's symbolic theory bases itself on both, as being related. The implications of this will be drawn out after a general discussion of the uses of symbolism.

Signs are important for communication. Some signs are simple and obvious, such as a frown or a smile. But beyond natural signs such as these there are also artificial symbols, and this greatly widens the range of possibilities of communication. Any system of language, for instance, will be arbitrary, with no natural relation between the sounds it uses and what the sounds signify; but the acceptance of this artificial system makes possible precision and variety in communication. Precisely because such symbols are arbitrary and artificial are they capable of great flexibility and versatility, more so than natural symbols.

What of the relation between symbol and the thing symbolized?

> The symbol is something which is, or which has been, directly accessible to the senses; it can be seen or heard or handled. The thing symbolized is out of reach and is not subject to direct control; but it is of a deeper order of importance than the symbol. The two are never simply identical; they are always to be distinguished though they cannot always be divorced.[29]

One must also note that the symbol never exhausts the reality. The symbol is never the same as the thing symbolized—the two are incommensurable. However, one must take care to appraise the relation between the two accurately. There are two besetting errors which people make in this regard. The one is to see only the immediate object, while ignoring its symbolic significance; the other is to identify the two. The latter is idolatry; the former is the approach of the positivist.

In the task of communication symbols are used for a variety of purposes—to convey information, to exhort, to warn. They may be 'performatory utterances', as in the case of wedding vows; and there are ritual actions, often commemorative ones. Their common characteristic is that they are stylized, and their validity depends on the acceptance of their conventional element.

> Apart from such agreement or ordinance, there would be no special significance and efficacy in the acts themselves. Their significance and efficacy are acquired and not inherent characters.[30]

It is the concept of symbolism which Sir Walter finds valuable for understanding the ethical element in punishment. His general discussion of symbolism leads into a further development of his thoughts on punishment as symbol, in which the ideas he has already begun to discuss are reinforced and further developed.

The primitive and spontaneous reaction to aggression cannot of itself be rightly termed punishment: it is a 'pre-moral' impulse. Similarly when the reaction is prompted simply by the desire for self-protection. In this instance retaliation is prompted by fear rather than by anger, but neither emotion is of itself sufficient to justify designating the action it prompts as punishment. Some kind of moral overtones are required to justify this, some kind of appeal to the conscience. In effect, Sir Walter's concept of punishment derives much from theology.

> ... in theological tradition, *malum poenae* corresponds to *malum culpae*, which it *both reflects and counters*.[31]

This again is based on the presupposition of there being two orders of good or evil, the one 'external' and material and the other 'internal' and moral. These two orders bear some similarity to each other, but must also be carefully distinguished. They are not identical, and overt acts are to be assessed for their deeper significance. Thus, wrongdoing and its inflicted penalty are both evils, but they are not evils of the same order. Wrongdoing belongs to the first order, and hence is far more serious. Punishment is of the second order.

> A punishment always *consists* in imposition of an evil or evils of the second order, it can only *suggest* an evil or evils of the first order. Many of its features are determined simply by convention and will vary with changes in convention. It is not itself an automatic result of wrongdoing, nor is it a universally obligatory response to wrongdoing. Wrongdoing may be consummated or it may be annulled; but punishment can never itself achieve either consummation or annulment of wrong, though it suggests both.[32]

Punishment is, as it were, a kind of dramatic expression of something that is true at a much deeper level.

> In some appropriate ritual action, it represents or embodies two spiritual processes, the wrongdoing and its counteraction.[33]

It foreshadows or forcibly suggests the inherent outworking of the evil deed, that is, the consummation of deterioration. And in addition it foreshadows the pain of conscience which the wrongdoer will feel as and when he realizes the meaning of what he had done. Sir Walter uses the analogy of sacramental theology to illustrate this function of punishment. Punishment serves as 'an outward and visible sign of an inward and spiritual disgrace'.[34] This is effected in two ways, corresponding to the two different 'drives' which have been shown to underlie the concept of punishment. On the one hand, punishment seeks to forestall the consummation of wrongdoing, and hence serves as an inverted sacrament in relation to this. On the other hand, punishment aims at promoting the annulment of wrongdoing—in relation to this it is a straightforward sacrament. However, it is noted that this is not something automatic. Punishment may seek to forestall moral deterioration and promote penitence, but it requires some response from the wrongdoer for it to be effective—just as the sacraments, though not subjective, do call for a response from the person who receives them.

Sir Walter sees punishment as having three aims, based on this appreciation of the intrinsically ruinous character of wrongdoing and the need to counteract it. These are: for persons in authority to consolidate this attitude in themselves; for this understanding to be promulgated to the world at large; and for appreciation of it to be stimulated in the wrongdoer.

It is not enough just to embody indignation against the wrongdoer. Something more is required.

> This involves a 'creative attention' to the wrongdoer which cannot be wholly hostile. It cannot seek to lower him in the scale of human excellence, for that would be devilish. But it does seek to induce him to rue his deed through seeing it as it really is ... You may thwart, humiliate and enchain an evil will, but so long as it remains evil you have failed to *annul* it.[35]

Neither is it enough solely to edify society. Acceptance of such a view might lead one to be satisfied with the semblance of justice alone, without regard for the reality of it. The two should coincide or—to put it another way—an external sanction should reinforce and be reinforced by an internal sanction. If the two are divorced, the potential effectiveness of a given sanction is reduced and, more importantly, this would be a travesty of what is commonly understood by justice. It is important that the wrongdoer and his deed should be placed in their social context and not isolated, but it must be borne in mind that action taken against an offender is not merely a matter of social expediency. As has been shown, it is something quite proper in itself.

The two traditional approaches to criminological thought are readily appreciated by Sir Walter, and form the starting-point of his discussion. The concept of desert is basic to the retributive view; the desire to undo is particularly significant for the utilitarian. Each idea is seen to be valid and important, but neither is adequate if isolated from the other. This in effect has been the radical defect of most theories of punishment: an unwarranted one-sidedness, in which the inherent lack of balance constantly requires the reassertion of the neglected factor. The tendency is to oscillate between two extremes, to demand that punishment should be either retributive or utilitarian. Sir Walter's exposition makes it clear that both ideas, in due relation, are essential to the theory of punishment. And, although he does not specifically underline the fact that his theory overcomes the dichotomy, this is what is actually effected, and may be noted as a major contribution of his theory.

It is also of considerable importance to note how the symbolic theory obviates this dichotomy. There is no facile assertion that punishment is, simply, both these things. It is vital to maintain the distinction between the two concepts even when they are set in relation. Sir Walter asserts that punishment is not identical with the intrinsic outworking of wrongdoing; nor is it itself the movement of restoration, though it seeks to promote this. Punishment is identical with neither, but is symbolic of both. To state this more clearly, this is an assertion that punishment is symbolic of two *contrary* things. There is no attempt to assimilate the one drive to the other or to suggest that desert and undoing are more or less the same. How then can both be fairly interlinked?

The question of what punishment *is* is a vexed one. What is meant by the use of *is*? Sir Walter is concerned to say that *is* does not imply identity. Most theories of punishment do assert identity and this, as it happens, is the great pitfall of criminological thought. *To assert identity is in fact to necessitate a dichotomy*, since this attempts to make punishment stand in relation to one thing and one alone. But we have seen that it is improper to assume that there is only one thing for punishment to stand in relation to. There prove to be two basic drives underlying the question of punishment, neither of which may properly be neglected. And, since these two drives differ from each other, and indeed are contrary movements, punishment cannot be *identical* with both. Thus, to speak of punishment as symbolic is not just to assert that it stands in a less closely articulated relationship to something than if it were identical with it. This assertion is after all made twice, in relation to two different drives. Therefore this is but the negative though necessary side of a positive statement: that if punishment is symbolic ('not identical with . . . but symbolic of . . .') it may properly *stand in relation to more than one thing at the same time*.

Hypothetically, there could perhaps be three kinds of theories of punishment: one-to-one identity theories, one-to-one symbolic theories, and the twofold symbolic theory. The first says that punishment *is* one thing; the second that it symbolizes one thing; and the third asserts that punishment symbolizes two things. It is of great importance to realize that Sir Walter's theory is the third kind, not the second. Otherwise his theory would be a mere modification of the first kind, a more loosely articulated version of it, and thus it would still be prone to most of its defects. In particular, a one-to-one symbolic theory would not overcome the traditional dichotomy, in that it would neglect to take into account both drives. The full potential of the symbolic view of punishment is only realized when it is twofold, based on the twofold denial of identity that we have detailed.

Our criticism of most traditional theories is that, through positing identity, they render inevitable a dichotomy in criminological thought. One might add to this that to posit identity is inevitable if one fails to see that there are two orders of (both) good and evil. This is not an idealistic extra to Sir Walter's theory, but is its essential basis. Unless one sees another, more primary, order beyond what is immediately apparent, one has no basis for denying that punishment is the essential outworking of wrongdoing. If there were one order alone, what else could be the outworking of wrongdoing? Similarly with the other denial. Unless there were another order, punishment would in itself have to be the movement of undoing and restoration, rather than an instrument to promote this. And, if there were no other order, punishment would have to be both these things, itself, at the same time—both the consummation of wrongdoing and its undoing! This proves to be the *reductio ad absurdum* of identity theories of punishment. Either one falls into an impossible dichotomy—impossible because one may not justifiably neglect either of the drives underlying punishment. Or one finds oneself trying to assert that punishment is (identically) both of these things at the same time, and this proves to be sheer nonsense.

This is but another form of our previous affirmation that punishment is not itself a consequence of wrongdoing, but rather an instrument for dealing with the consequences of wrongdoing. These consequences lie in the first order, that of moral being. Punishment is of the second order, and must not be equated with anything of the first order. The fact of there being two orders rules out the possibility of identity theories of punishment, and it is the attempt to express the relationship between the two orders which is the contribution of the symbolic theory. We have suggested that a mature theory of punishment is marked by its concern for the disposition of the wrongdoer. The question then raised is that of accessibility, of how something may be done to affect the wrongdoer's disposition. Punishment as something inflicted may thus be spoken of as a means of access, or an instrument by which the relation between the two orders is affected. In this sense, neither punishment nor infliction should be seen with any overtones of animosity. The statement of their purpose is intended as something factual and not emotive.

In sum, what we must bear in mind is that the theory of punishment does rest on certain essential presuppositions, which are often neglected altogether when not specifically stated. These are: that there are two orders, the moral and the material; that wrongdoing sets in train certain consequences in the moral order, namely, the process of moral deterioration; that, given that it is desirable to arrest this process, there arises the problem of how this moral order may be affected; that thus an instrument is required which provides access to, and is capable of promoting a change in, this order; and that in effect a twofold change is here required—moral deterioration or continuing impenitence is to be forestalled, and restoration to goodness or penitence is to be promoted. This is the context in which punishment is to be considered, and which the symbolic theory does take into account.

Moreover, to acknowledge the difference between the two orders, and to stress that punishment is not identical with the consequences of wrongdoing, provides a safeguard against determinism—a kind of 'distancing' which identity theories of their very nature cannot provide. Punishment is instrument and not goal; and, further, no claim is made for it as an infallible instrument. It may forestall intransigence and it may promote penitence, but it is not bound to do either, because even the provision of genuine access to the moral order is not to overrule freedom of choice.

Sir Walter makes use of the analogy of pain as a warning-signal in the biological sphere for our understanding of punishment. He says:

> ... a child may learn prudence by experiencing the results of imprudence; if he is careless with his knife, he cuts his finger.[36]

But,

If the natural physical consequences of imprudent action are sometimes quite disastrous, we must devise some other means of conveying the lesson.[37]

Several suggestions may be made in connection with this. One sees that a limited amount of pain in the biological sphere may serve to warn against more serious physical consequences. For the ethical sphere this would imply that a limited amount of 'suffering' (not necessarily *pain* as such) may serve to warn against more serious moral consequences. This parallels what Sir Walter says of the attempt to check the process of moral deterioration, which would ultimately be disastrous for the wrongdoer. Punishment might thus be seen as a kind of immunization, the idea of which is that a small dose now will forestall a more serious bout of the real thing later. Or punishment may be said to serve as an antidote, in counteracting the process of deterioration. Whether or not the specific terms 'immunization' and 'antidote' are particularly helpful, it would seem that there is a useful analogy to be drawn here between the biological and the moral spheres.

In addition, the biological analogy does also provide us with a clear indication of the value of such a warning-signal. To lack the capacity to feel pain is the condition of the leper, who through this inability undergoes bodily mutilation, thanks to being unable to assess accurately whether or not a situation or action is physically harmful. Anaesthesia is, in the long run, extremely dangerous; and, on the given analogy, moral anaesthesia would probably be equally destructive. As we noted at the beginning of our inquiry into suffering, the goal is not the cessation of suffering *per se*, which might in effect be equated with anaesthesia. The goal is one of putting things to right in the moral sphere, or the restoration of interdependence. This might eventually obviate actual suffering, but the capacity for suffering is never lost. To lose this ability would be to undermine the very dynamic of interdependence, and thus the smaller loss—of this capacity— would be catastrophic through betokening a far larger loss, of the goal that actually is desired.

The fact that punishment aims at forestalling the ruinous moral consequences of wrongdoing leads us to note another, paradoxical, point: that, strictly speaking, punishment is *not* to give a person his due. It has been pointed out that a wrongdoer's only due, in the strict sense, is moral deterioration. But the task of punishment is to try to forestall this, or, in other words, to *prevent* a person from attaining what is due to him. Not only is punishment not to give due, but in fact due cannot be *given* by anything; one can only leave the wrongdoer to attain it, as he will unless he undergoes a change of heart. We need to bear in mind that punishment is something external, of the second order, and that the wrongdoer's due is a matter of moral being, i.e. in the first order. Punishment may provide access to the first order, for our attempt to modify it, but it is itself to be carefully distinguished from it. The relation of punishment to due or desert is not one of identification, as is supposed by one type of identity theory. The demand for punishment is sometimes expressed by the cry of 'Give him his due!' What we wish to make clear is that to do this is literally impossible, since due cannot be *given*, and moreover the aim of *punishment* is precisely to forestall the attainment of the wrongdoer's due. In any case desert is but one of two drives underlying the idea of punishment, and so we come to reaffirm the twofold and symbolic character of punishment. One might also note, in order to avoid possible confusion, that we are contrasting 'giving due' with 'forestalling due'. No suggestion is being made that, if punishment is not to give due, it is to give what is not due. There can be no question of this.

Punishment is not merely to secure a future end of restoration but is to transform the would-be future end of a past act, that is, moral deterioration. There is an outcome to be forestalled as well as an outcome to be promoted, and it would thus be misleading to speak of 'the goal' of punishment, as if there were only one goal. Restoration certainly presupposes the forestalling of intransigence, but this forestalling is a distinct element, and may sometimes occur apart from restoration, i.e. there may be mere deterrence, or the partially modified consequences of wrongdoing. To speak simply of the goal of restoration is also likely to lead to overemphasis on only one of the two drives underlying punishment: in this instance, the desire to undo rather than the demand for desert. And, because restoration is to be promoted, it might well become difficult to give due weight to the essential forestalling character of punishment, unless one specifically kept in sight what it is that punishment is to forestall (certainly not restoration!).

The two drives underlying the theory of punishment have been spoken of in various ways, which may be conveniently summarized. The concept of desert has been set beside the desire for undoing. The movement of continuation in the state of wrong is contrasted with the move towards counteraction. On the one hand, there is the possibility of the consummation of moral deterioration, or intransigence, which is to be forestalled. On the other hand, there is the possibility of undoing or transforming the moral consequences of wrongdoing in the person of the wrongdoer; this is penitence, or the move to restoration, which is to be promoted. Moral deterioration and penitence are the two referents of punishment, the two things to which punishment stands in a certain instrumental relation. These two drives are *both* in the first order, of moral being. Punishment is something external; it belongs to the second order, and aims at providing access to its two referents in the first order. The twofold character of punishment (forestalling and promoting) derives from the two underlying drives of desert and undoing. The perennial temptation is to minimize the importance of one or the other, or to assume that neither can be given proper emphasis without ignoring the other. Hence the dichotomies and confusion of much criminological thought. Hence too the need to reassess basic principles, and so to reconstruct the theory of punishment from within its essential context.

The model of the two orders is also helpful in elucidating the problem of incommensurability, which is so often raised in connection with the theory of punishment. It is generally attempted to ensure that punishment is in some way proportionate to the antecedent act of wrongdoing. Equally, it may be pointed out that punishment and wrongdoing are not strictly commensurable. As a corollary to this, it is sometimes assumed that any attempt at proportionality is misguided. This rests on the assumption that wrongdoing and punishment ought to be commensurable and that, if they are not, there cannot be any real justice in punishment. This is an unnecessary piece of confusion. One may agree that wrongdoing and punishment are not strictly commensurable, but it is mistaken to demand that they should be so. One is not to try in this way to measure something in the first order (wrongdoing) against something in the second order (punishment). There are two commensurables, but they are both in the same order—

the first order. Wrongdoing and punishment may not be commensurable, but wrongdoing *and moral deterioration* are very strictly commensurable. (It is this that is the true fulfilment of the 'similarity' of the *lex talionis* idea.) Thus, the actual question of commensurability is a proper one, but has generally been asked with reference to the wrong pair of data. Hence of course there has been distortion and difficulty in any answer given to it. What is commensurable with wrongdoing is its consequence of moral deterioration, which it is the task of punishment to forestall. Punishment is interposed between these two true commensurables, as an instrument for dealing with the consequences of wrongdoing. In that punishment is symbolic of, and referential to, the whole process of what is happening in the first order, it will assume some form of at least rough proportionality to it. But the demand for strict commensurability is quite improper. Wrongdoing and punishment are not commensurables, *nor are they intended to be so*.

In speaking of Sir Walter's theory as symbolic, we are not intending to suggest that it is a merely 'proclamatory' theory. It is sometimes suggested that punishment functions as a means of expressing society's disapproval, and that this is its chief or sole function. In this way punishment is seen as something 'proclamatory' or 'denunciatory'.[38] These are in effect minimalist theories. They claim little, and for this very reason are of little use for one's understanding of punishment. Sir Walter's understanding of punishment does *derive* from his consideration of the meaning of ritual and ceremonial actions, namely the lasting impression made on him by the account of the Dreyfus case. However, this has proved to be simply a starting-point for something fuller and more profound. Symbolism provides the key for assessment of the ethical element in punishment; and punishment as symbol is regarded not as merely descriptive, but as actually efficacious. Punishment, as an instrument for transforming the consequences of wrongdoing in the person of the wrongdoer, may also *in so doing* express the attitude of society towards wrongdoing and the wrongdoer. But if the expression of disapproval is all that is desired, punishment is superfluous—and the consequences of wrongdoing remain unaffected.

The symbolic character of punishment consists in its twofold reference beyond itself, its referential character. And a referent is

## THE SYMBOLIC THEORY OF PUNISHMENT 81

always greater than the symbol that expresses or represents it. Punishment is merely an instrument, though an important instrument. It may be a form of 'suffering' or at any rate constraint of the guilty, but it points beyond itself to suffering as understood in terms of moral being, i.e. to moral deterioration and to penitence. These are the kinds of suffering that are most intimately linked with the actual personality. This is not to suggest that second-order suffering is unreal or unimportant, but its significance lies beyond itself, in what it refers to. Just because symbolism as such is something artificial and conventional (understood in a factual and not pejorative sense), one is not to focus on the symbol to the neglect of what is symbolized. Thus, the symbolic theory is based on the recognition that there can be no understanding of guilty suffering within punishment unless one has reached an understanding of what guilty suffering means independently of punishment.

# 6

# The Reassessment of Criminological Thought

In the light of the preceding two chapters we should now be in a position to re-evaluate criminological thought generally. This will at the same time reinforce the conclusions drawn from our examination of Sir Walter Moberly's thought. His theory will be our critical apparatus, our new perspective. Thus, we shall now consider some aspects of the development of the two main schools of criminological thought—the retributive and the utilitarian—while bearing in mind that this traditional dichotomy may no longer claim our acceptance.

## THE RETRIBUTIVE SCHOOL

Although it has suffered a considerable loss of support in recent years, the retributive approach has been championed by some of the major philosophers of modern times. One of the foremost of these has been Immanuel Kant. In a discussion of the right of punishing, he states:

> Juridical punishment can never be administered merely as a means for promoting another good, either with regard to the criminal himself or to civil society, but must in all cases be imposed only because the individual on whom it is inflicted *has committed a crime*. For one man ought never to be dealt with merely as a means subservient to the purpose of another ... He must first be found guilty and *punishable*, before there can be any thought of drawing from his punishment any benefit for himself or his fellow citizens. The penal law is a categorical imperative, and woe to him who creeps through the serpent-windings of utilitarianism to discover some advantage that may discharge him from the justice of punishment.[1]

It is emphasized here that punishment is not to be used as an instrument for furthering purposes unrelated to its own justification. This has been the persistent insight of the retributive approach, not to rule out other purposes, but to insist that they may be considered *only* when derivative from the primary justification of punishment, and *only* when this primary justification is and remains granted. We may reiterate what Kant has said about this justification with the words of F. H. Bradley:

> Punishment is punishment, only where it is deserved. We pay the penalty, because we owe it, and for no other reason; and if punishment is inflicted for any other reason whatever than because it is merited by wrong, it is a gross immorality, a crying injustice, an abominable crime, and not what it pretends to be.[2]

While agreeing with this basic emphasis we must at the same time be critical of the traditional retributive approach. We must take into account both what retributivism is and, just as importantly, what it is not. We may do this by examining a selection of modern retributive statements in the light of the conclusions we have already drawn from Sir Walter's theory.

*Punishment in general is physical evil accruing from moral evil.*[3] Punishment is physical evil (though not necessarily pain as such), and it does attempt to deal with the moral evil of wrongdoing. But although it is subsequent to wrongdoing, it is not itself a consequence of wrongdoing in the strict sense. The only thing that may properly be said to *accrue* to the wrongdoer from moral evil is further moral evil, i.e. moral deterioration.

*Retribution is inflicted on the criminal.*[4] This must be denied. Punishment is inflicted on the criminal, but punishment is not retribution. Rather, retribution—the true, intrinsic retribution of moral deterioration—is precisely what punishment attempts to halt as a process and forestall short of its consummation. (Nobody can *inflict* retribution in any case; one can only leave a person to attain it.)

*... punishment (is) the infliction of pain on a person because he has done wrong.*[5] True, but this kind of statement is compatible with differing views of the underlying justification of punishment, and hence may be misleading. The infliction of pain on a person because he has done wrong is not to be understood as the retribution of wrongdoing: punishment is not and cannot be the infliction of retribution. Rather, it presupposes that there is

retribution, because the doing of wrong has started or furthered a process of moral deterioration in the wrongdoer. This it seeks to turn the wrongdoer from.

*... if a man has done wrong it is right and just that he should suffer for it.*[6] Yes, but this is primarily true of moral being, and refers to what is intrinsic and not to what is imposed by decision. Only in a secondary sense may it refer to punishment. However, if a man has done wrong and is thus in a process of moral deterioration, it is good that something should be done to attempt to transform the consequences of wrongdoing in him.

*Retribution is supported ... on the ground that it is just.*[7] This is another statement which is made to refer to punishment in its original context. But punishment and retribution are not to be thus identified. And, although punishment may be granted or denied our support, the retribution that is moral deterioration is simply the entail of wrongdoing in the personality. It is not a matter for our support or otherwise, since its occurrence is not optional or a matter of imposition.

*... to preserve some relation between immorality and suffering.*[8] In its given context this forms part of a statement that not all retributivists would justify punishment by this principle alone. Of interest for our purpose is its suggestion that anyone should seek to make this the purpose of punishment. Punishment is not to preserve some relation between immorality and suffering. Moral deterioration is inevitably entailed by wrongdoing, i.e. there is already some relation between immorality and suffering. Punishment does not *create* this. It presupposes this, and may indeed remind us of this; but the purpose of punishment is not to preserve or reinforce the relation, but to transform it.

It should become evident from these comments that traditional retributive statements are not usually capable of drawing the vital distinction between punishment and the intrinsic retribution of wrongdoing, which is moral deterioration, a referent of punishment. There is particular confusion in the use of the terms 'desert' and 'deserved'. The wrongdoer deserves punishment; but punishment is not, in the sense commonly understood, the 'desert' of the wrongdoer. From our discussion of Sir Walter Moberly's theory, it should by now be clear that, in its truest and most proper sense, the desert of the wrongdoer is moral deterioration. Punishment *refers* to this, but is certainly not to be equated with it. The task of *punishment* is, as we have seen, to forestall this desert. The person who is subject to the moral consequences of wrongdoing *deserves* to be treated with the instrument of second-order suffering that attempts to check this process of deterioration and to promote his restoration to goodness. In this way we may expand and see the meaning of the statement that 'punishment is deserved'. It is easy to understand how hitherto there has been confusion on this point. The similarity of terminology has marked not merely linguistic confusion, but has been based on a genuine inability to distinguish between punishment and its referent. When punishment was, improperly, identified with retribution, it was natural to speak of punishment as the 'desert' of the wrongdoer. But this identification was wrong, and hence statements deriving from such identification are incorrect. First-order suffering and second-order suffering are not to be equated.

It would seem that the chief difficulty in retributive thought hitherto has been the absence of the model of the two orders, which would provide a clear basis for distinguishing between punishment and its referents. Short of this, retributive theory may speak of punishment, of retribution, and even of annulment, but the inter-relation of these concepts remains ambiguous. Sir Walter Moberly's theory owes much to the Hegelians, indeed it might perhaps be considered a radical development of the Hegelian approach. But while Hegelian thought may have provided a matrix for the development of the symbolic theory, in itself it would seem, from the point of view of this later development, to be subject to the ambiguity of inter-relation we have just spoken of. Hegel and the Hegelian school of British Idealists are retributivists. However, Hegel's insistence on a retributive approach is combined with a considerable emphasis on annulment, and this is maintained in the retributive approach of such philosophers as Bradley and Bosanquet. What it would seem that Hegel and the Hegelians are attempting to say is this: that both retribution and annulment are valid concepts. But at this point the difficulty arises. Each of these ideas may be valid, but what is their mutual relation? A premature solution would be either to overstate one at the expense of the other, or to attempt to equate the two. This would not do justice to the fact that both concepts are valid, and that they are in contrast with each other, as Sir Walter Moberly's analysis has emphasized. A more significant difficulty lies in the fact that it is attempted to make each and both of these statements true of punishment in itself. But both are, as we have seen, descriptive of moral being, that is to say, the character of the wrongdoer, which punishment may be used as an instrument to influence. Both are to be understood as referents of punishment, rather than as punishment itself. Thus, we may not agree with Hegel that 'the annulment of the crime is retribution'.[9] Annulment and retribution may not be equated; and neither together nor individually may they be identified with punishment itself. Again, in speaking of punishment, Hegel says that 'retribution is inflicted on the criminal'.[10] We have already pointed out that, although punishment is inflicted on the criminal, punishment is not retribution.[11] Likewise, we may not straightforwardly accept Bosanquet's statement that 'the principle of annulment ... is the ground and nature of punishment'.[12] Punishment attempts to promote annulment—the annulment that is reformation—but punishment is not itself that annulment. And annulment itself is only one of the two referents of punishment: the given remark overstates one side of the dichotomy and therefore fails to do justice to the fact of there being two drives underlying the question of punishment.

It will also be useful to bear in mind that we are discussing personality, and not abstract right and wrong. When Hegel speaks of punishment as being 'to annul the crime, which otherwise would have been held valid',[13] the phrase 'would have been held valid' is perhaps unduly abstract from the point of view of the symbolic theory. If punishment is not applied, or if it does not succeed in its purpose, the entail of wrongdoing remains. This is the way in which we may understand the given statement. To translate this into terms of 'upholding the validity of the crime' is an impersonal mode of speaking, and may even mark a definite lack of appreciation of the consequences of wrongdoing in and for the personality. Hegel goes on to say:

> ... crime is to be annulled, not because it is the producing of an evil, but because it is an infringement of the right as right.[14]

On our understanding, however, it is the producing of evil that is of concern here—the evil of moral deterioration—and it is precisely this that needs to be tackled. Likewise, to speak of punishment as 'the nullity of (a) nullity',[15] while characteristic of the Hegelian approach, is insufficiently personalist for the symbolic understanding, and again risks laying too much stress on the second of punishment's first-order referents, namely, annulment. Here, as previously, it is important to distinguish punishment from its referents. It and they are not to be identified. We should add, though, that in saying this we are not attempting to attack the Hegelian dialectic as such. Our aim is solely to point out its shortcomings in the sphere of criminological thought.

Although lacking the theoretical basis of the model of the two orders, the Hegelians do in practice make some distinction between punishment and the annulment it is to promote. Bosanquet speaks of how pain may bring us to our senses,[16] and McTaggart comments:

> Hegel's theory is that punishment, that is, pain inflicted because the sufferer had previously done wrong, may lead to repentance for the crime which caused the punishment ... The thesis is not that it always produces repentance—which, of course, is not the case—but that there is something in its nature which tends to produce repentance.[17]

The hope of annulment is the hope of reformation: not a merely abstract cancellation of wrong, but personal amendment. Interestingly, we have reached this conclusion while still within a discussion of the retributive approach. The fundamentally reformative idea of annulment is an integral part of the Hegelian school of thought. This differs from the utilitarian approach chiefly in its insistence on desert, guilt, or blameworthiness, as being essential to the justification of punishment. Without this, punishment must be regarded as meaningless. Other considerations are 'external to the matter, they can not give us a right to punish, and nothing can do that but criminal desert'.[18] However, once this essential matter of priorities has been established, other considerations may legitimately be taken into account. 'Having once the right to punish, we may modify the punishment according to the useful and the pleasant.'[19] This should not be understood as an apologetic qualification or concession, still less as a confusion of two different principles. I would suggest that we may use language even stronger than Bradley's, and state that 'having once the right to punish, we should determine the punishment according to the useful and the pleasant'. If one grants the retributive principle that wrongdoing has (moral) consequences for the wrongdoer; and if one understands punishment as an instrument for transforming these consequences in the person of the wrongdoer; it then becomes natural to shape the form of the punishment according to whatever will be of most use in furthering the transformation of the consequences of wrongdoing. In other words, it is the very concept of retribution that leads one to utilitarian considerations: these are not opposed to the acceptance of retribution, nor should they be divorced from it. They are, properly, derivative from it.

Subsequent to the Hegelians, the retributive approach has met with increasing disfavour, and by the second half of the twentieth century we find retributivists placed on the defensive. The 1950s saw the attempt to establish the retributive understanding of punishment by making it a matter of definition: logical rather than moral considerations were placed to the fore. Unfortunately, the matter was not so easily to be settled. Moreover, definitions along the lines of 'punishment is the infliction of pain on the guilty' were criticized as unable to cover cases of punishment inflicted on persons who were in fact innocent. To have altered this to 'punishment ought to be the infliction of pain on the guilty' would have meant a shift away from the safety of verbal recommendation back to the battleground of moral proposals and justifications. The symbolic approach would seem to involve both logical and moral elements. The case of mistaken punishment would be covered as follows: Punishment is an instrument for dealing with the consequences of wrongdoing in the person of the wrongdoer. As such, it ought to be applied only to the persons for whom it is—by definition—intended, namely, wrongdoers. However, the fact that it may sometimes in practice be mistakenly or improperly applied does not in any way impugn the validity of the given definition. It *is* such-and-such an instrument, by definition; and it *ought* to be applied in such-and-such a way—a moral proposal based on our statement of definition. The old definition, that 'punishment is the infliction of pain on the guilty', was inadequate as a descriptive statement, as not always being factually true. What plausibility it had may have been due to a hidden prescriptive element, something along the lines of: 'Punishment—if it is applied as it ought to be applied—is the infliction of pain on the guilty.' On the symbolic theory we may take such a statement as: 'He was punished for what he did not do' and render it alternatively: 'The instrument for dealing with the consequences of wrongdoing in the person of the wrongdoer was applied to someone who had not done wrong.' This is, of course, the description of an unfortunate occurrence; but it is not a logically contradictory statement. The definition as such holds good.

Another shortcoming of definitional retributivism has been the tendency to reduce guilt to a limiting principle, and to make it a necessary rather than a sufficient condition for punishment, i.e. we should not punish the innocent, but it is not necessarily assumed that we *should* punish the guilty. This may be exemplified by certain recent statements.

> ... the criminal law's traditional emphasis on blameworthiness as a prerequisite to the imposition of punishment ... is a *limiting* principle, not a justification for action. It is wrong to say that we should punish persons simply because they commit offenses under circumstances that we can call blameworthy. It is right to say that we should not punish those who commit offenses unless we can say that their conduct is blameworthy.[20]

Also,

> There no longer are defenders of the traditional retribution theory, or at least of the version that we are obliged rather than permitted to punish offenders because they deserve it.[21]

This restriction of blameworthiness would seem to rest on an insufficient appreciation of the consequences of wrongdoing. To impute blameworthiness is not merely to assert that someone has committed a wrongful act. The act of wrongdoing has inaugurated or reinforced a process of moral deterioration; it has had repercussions on the personality of the wrongdoer. It would certainly be improper to apply the instrument for dealing with the consequences of wrongdoing to someone who has not done wrong and hence is not subject to the entail of wrongdoing. One is not to punish a non-wrongdoer. But to decide not to punish someone who is a wrongdoer will generally mean leaving that person subjected to the entail of wrongdoing, by not applying the instrument that would attempt to transform this. One may choose whether or not to impose the second-order suffering of punishment, but the first-order suffering of moral deterioration is not optional. Blameworthiness implies that there is a situation that needs to be remedied. The true insight of the retributive approach is not that punishment is retributive, but that there is such a thing as retribution and that punishment is to be applied in an attempt to deal with this.

## THE UTILITARIAN SCHOOL

The classical deterrent approach to punishment was shaped in reaction to the capriciousness and employment of savage penalties that had developed by the late seventeenth century. The acceptance of secret accusations and inadequate evidence, the use of torture, and the multiplication of crimes subject to capital punishment—all this was recognized as inhumane and in need of drastic reform. Foremost amongst those calling for reform was the Italian, Beccaria. In his work *Of Crimes and Punishments* (1764)[22] he characterizes the purpose of punishment as being to prevent the wrongdoer from further injuring his fellow citizens, and to deter others from committing similar offences; the aim is not the mere infliction of pain on the offender. In practice, the certainty of punishment will be a more effective deterrent than severity; no more pain should be inflicted than necessary. Above all, it is better to prevent crimes than to punish them. The principle underlying this approach is specifically that of utilitarian philosophy: 'The greatest happiness of the greatest number'. The aim of legislation is to lead people to the greatest possible happiness or the least possible misery, according to the calculation of all the goods and evils of life (the 'felicific calculus'). This approach is further developed in the writings of Jeremy Bentham.

If Beccaria is the Luther of this 'new reformation', Bentham is its Calvin, its chief systematic theologian. It is to him that we look for the fullest and clearest exposition of the new doctrine.[23]

As a utilitarian, Bentham is committed to stressing the influence on men's actions of pleasure and pain:

Nature has placed mankind under the governance of two sovereign masters, *pain* and *pleasure*.[24]

And again, to underline this point:

But whether it be this or anything else that is to be *done*, there is nothing by which a man can ultimately be *made* to do it, but either pain or pleasure.[25]

A number of criticisms arise, and indeed have already arisen, in connection with this kind of approach. First, we may suggest that pain might be considered the ultimate evil only for a merely biological organism, devoid of the capacity for moral choice that is characteristic of human personality. Pain is in itself physical evil; but there is such a thing as moral evil as well, which is arguably the more serious. Moreover, even as a physical phenomenon, pain is not an unqualified evil, even if unpleasant. It serves as a warning-signal of damage to the body, and thus attempts to alert one to and forestall the greater physical evil of bodily deterioration and destruction.

Second, the insistence on pleasure and pain leads all too readily to a 'stick and carrot' approach to conduct, and a lack of appreciation of the intrinsic value of good and evil. Even without any mercenary overtones, the bestowal of pleasure and the avoidance of pain may only be regarded as 'interim motivations'. To denote them thus is not to condemn them—they serve a useful and important role in society as it is—but they should be seen for what they are. They are at best instrumental, and not ends in themselves. Ultimately and most fundamentally, we may suggest that goodness and happiness do coincide, and that happiness is a quality proper to goodness. Similarly with badness and unhappiness. However, so long as a distinction may be drawn between the two terms of each of these pairs, it would be mistaken to regard either the pursuit of happiness or the avoidance of unhappiness as unqualified goals. In practice, we often do not have an immediate appreciation of the value of the good and the bad, and hence need some help towards this. Thus, to reward a good act should be a means of *drawing attention to* the intrinsic value and desirability of the good act—assuming that we have not yet learned to see this in and for itself. Unfortunately in practice a reward may result in goodness being understood as a means to (another) happiness, rather than as of itself possessing this quality. In theory a reward should point *to*, and not away *from*, the innate quality of goodness. And ultimately the need for reward would be superseded, if the understanding of goodness as being its own reward were fully realized. To *bestow* a reward on goodness is basically an 'interim' measure.

Likewise the inability to recognize the true nature of the link between badness and suffering has led to considerable confusion in the theory of punishment. The suffering stemming from the very nature of wrongdoing, and the suffering that is imposed in an attempt to check this, must be carefully distinguished from each other. Moreover, although badness and suffering are linked, not all suffering is indicative of badness. On the contrary, a good person may suffer, and his suffering should not be taken to impugn the quality of his goodness. This in turn reflects on the nature of the link between goodness and reward. The righteous may be rewarded, but the reward is not definitive or constitutive of their righteousness, and neither is it possible nor would it be desirable for the righteous only to be rewarded. Rewards should serve and be subservient to the promotion of goodness; and goodness in the midst of suffering is still its own reward.

We may see from this that a pleasure-and-pain ethic runs the risk of prematurely absolutizing the link between goodness and happiness, and badness and unhappiness. The real link is an intrinsic one, *compatible with any external conditions, whether or not these happen to reflect this inherent bond*. Alternatively, such an ethic may lead to the divorce of the qualities referred to, so that happiness is preferred to goodness, and the avoidance of unhappiness preferred to the avoidance of badness. These are the hazards of what is essentially an interim ethic, if the limitations of its provisional nature are not recognized. The utilitarian position would not seem to take this sufficiently into account.

Despite these shortcomings in the overall theory of utilitarianism, it is undeniable that its application in the sphere of criminology has been of great benefit and has led to substantial improvements in penal systems. Unfortunately, the right and necessary opposition to practical abuses was on the theoretical level equated with the rejection of retributive theory. And so for two centuries the utilitarian and retributive approaches have been generally defined in contrast to each other, rather than as truly complementary. J. S. Mill was led to say:

> There are two ends which ... are sufficient to justify punishment: the benefit of the offender himself, and the protection of others.[26]

On our own understanding, any good retributivist should have been able to say this as well.

In the course of time there have been some shifts of emphasis in the utilitarian approach to criminology. Although originally linked with specifically utilitarian philosophy, utilitarian criminology has in the course of the twentieth century been largely detached from this larger field of reference. It is now defined by its emphasis on the consequences of punishment, rather than by subscription to the classical statements of utilitarian philosophy.

> Utilitarianism holds that punishment must always be justified by the value of its consequences. I shall refer to this as 'utility' for convenience without any implication that utility must consist in pleasure. The view that punishment is justified by the value of its consequences is compatible with any ethical theory which allows meaning to be attached to moral judgements.[27]

The emphasis on the consequences of punishment, without understanding these to be the transformed consequences of wrongdoing, has led to exclusively forward-looking theories of punishment. Retrospective theories have been rejected, and the possibility of accepting any kind of retributive approach has been reduced, and for some ruled out altogether.

Another, more acceptable, modification has been the increasing emphasis on the need for reformation, as distinct from mere deterrence. This was not, of course, entirely absent from the thought of earlier utilitarians. We find Jeremy Bentham saying:

> It is a great merit in a punishment to contribute to the reformation of the offender, not only through fear of being punished again, but by a change in his character and habits.[28]

But it would seem fair to say, first, that the primary model for early utilitarian thought was that of deterrence; and, second, that the twentieth century has seen the growth of an unprecedented concern with reformation.

The utilitarian approach contains much that is attractive, in particular its humane concern for offenders. This was something that was lacking in much of traditional retributivism, and the deficiency urgently needed making good. However, we cannot accept utilitarian theory without qualification. Its root limitation lies in its divorce from the retributive school, and a variety of defects stem from this separation. It has, for instance, been said that:

The idea that no man can deserve to suffer, and that the justification of punishment is to be found only in its utility is common to all the utilitarians.[29]

In other words, the chief effect of defining utilitarianism in opposition to retributivism has been the rejection of the concept of desert. The practical motivation behind this may originally have been humane, but the implications of it are alarming. By what right may one deprive a man of his liberty, and subject him to reformative treatment, if this is not *deserved*? For whether or not one describes this process as punishment, in substance it remains the same as what we would understand as punishment: it is suffering, even if it does not involve pain.

The mere deprivation of liberty, however benign the administration of the place of confinement, is undeniably punishment.[30]

Similarly,

Measures which subject individuals to the substantial and involuntary deprivation of their liberty are essentially punitive in character, and this reality is not altered by the fact that the motivations that prompt incarceration are to provide therapy or otherwise contribute to the person's well-being or reform.[31]

Thus, by asserting that wrongdoers do not *deserve* to suffer, the utilitarians are exposing themselves to the criticism of advocating *un*deserved suffering. Not to mention the possibility of punishing the non-wrongdoer, which—as many are already aware—might well be 'justified' by the utilitarian approach. This is even more evidently undeserved suffering, but here we are simply pointing out that for the utilitarian even the punishment of the wrongdoer may, on his own principles, have to be understood as undeserved suffering.

It would seem that utilitarian practice has been better than utilitarian theory, but it is important to insist on clarifying the implications of utilitarian theory, and to call for the rejection of unacceptable developments. The desire to eliminate vindictiveness from the practice of punishment must not be translated back into theory as the rejection of the concept of desert. Otherwise, humane intentions may in turn lead to the justification of further inhumanity.

An extreme development of this repugnance for the idea of desert has been the call to abandon the concept of responsibility. Advocates of 'social defence' wish to treat a wrongdoer without holding him responsible.[32] This kind of approach 'denies the existence of responsibility based on "guilt" freely incurred and hence the justification of "punishment" '.[33] The theoretical rejection of punishment would not seem to make much practical difference, however. The State is still to intervene in the life of the given person, and either to reform him or to confine him if unreformable.[34] To speak of this as non-retributive does not seem to be justifiable. Either the given individual has shown himself to be delinquent, in which case intervention *is* retributive, in that it is based on this fact. Or an individual has not shown himself to be delinquent, in which case there is no need, or justification, for such intervention.

In any case, it is perhaps not sufficiently realized that the deterrent theory would seem to include a version of the retributive theory within itself. It has been said, for instance, that:

> The strongest utilitarian case for punishment is that it serves to deter potential offenders by inflicting suffering on actual ones.[35]

A statement like this assumes that it is desirable to maintain *a link between wrongdoing and suffering* in the mind of all concerned. But what is this link if not the essence of the retributive position? Likewise McTaggart, in speaking of the deterrent view of punishment:

> ... its main object is deterrent—to prevent crime by making the possible criminal afraid of the punishment *which would follow.*[36]

But how can it be stated that punishment 'would follow' crime, if a retributive approach is not implicitly presupposed? And why should suffering deter people *from* crime, if in fact it is not connected *with* crime? The deterrent theory as commonly stated is unable to avoid making some sort of link between the two factors, and this link needs to be seen as involving an essentially retributive position. The statements just quoted may overtly cast the deterrent theory in the form of a *prediction* of the retributive theory; but they do not obviate the retributive approach altogether. And even as statements of present fact, as distinct from predictions of future fact, they still presuppose a retributive understanding, in that they are basing future deterrence on the *present* maintenance of a link between wrongdoing and penal suffering.

Deterrent theory may also be subject to other criticisms. It has been suggested that the pursuit of deterrence or of reformation may justify the indefinite or even lifelong deprivation of a person's freedom:

> The vital element of the possibility of lifelong incarceration if the individual is shown by scientific investigation to require it, may reasonably be expected to reinforce the natural deterrent effect of the threat of punishment.[37]

But is this not far more severe than what was allowed by retributive theory? It may be doubted whether either criminals themselves or the moral instincts of society in general would wish to accept this kind of development in preference to a retributive approach. The most likely objection to be raised is quite simply that this would not be *just* (with the implication that justice is being thwarted by injustice, rather than that it is being commuted on grounds of mercy). The importance of justice as a yardstick is not to be underestimated. It may not be easy to elucidate what justice is; but it is more readily possible to point to what is manifestly unjust. Indeed, this was the utilitarians' own starting-point, in reaction to the excesses of penal practice in their day.

Current utilitarian theory is also held to allow of the possibility of high penalties generally, or proportionately higher penalties for smaller crimes, in order to maximize their deterrent value. The irony of history is that this is precisely the thing that the utilitarian reformers were originally protesting against! The harsh penalties of their time were realized to be both unjust and ineffective. The practice of high penalties for small crimes may be epitomized by the well-known proverb, 'as well be hanged for a sheep as a lamb', which was once no metaphor. The severity of penalties at times led to the refusal to convict persons known to be guilty, precisely because penalties were considered quite disproportionate to the crime. Unduly high penalties were, and would still be, ineffective deterrents. It was the uncritical application of the retributive approach that once led to these abuses, and this was challenged by the utilitarians. Now the position would seem to be reversed. Unthinking utilitarianism is in danger of sanctioning the kind of abuses it once criticized, and it is the retributive contribution to try and check this. It is our contention that deterrence properly stems from the retributive approach and, conversely, needs to remain grounded in it. Either aspect when divorced from the other is shown to be capable of sanctioning abuses. Indeed it would seem that both may sanction the same kind of abuses. Both approaches, the utilitarian and the retributive, need to remain subject to scrutiny.

The aim is to deter or reform a *wrongdoer*. Without this retributive caveat, it could be suggested that it might be useful to punish the innocent. To do this would be a meaningless exercise, as well as immoral, since people who have not committed wrong are not subject to its entail, and hence do not need to be treated with an instrument that attempts to transform the entail of wrongdoing. Not only this, but in the absence of a retributive matrix utilitarians also tend to find it difficult to see the point of punishing the guilty. The possibilities of punishing the innocent, and of not punishing the guilty, are alike the corollaries of a utilitarianism that is insufficiently grounded in retributivism.

The chief factor that has led to questioning the punishment of the guilty would seem to be a lack of appreciation of the consequences of wrongdoing—the fact that there is in some degree an existing situation of moral deterioration, which it is desirable that punishment should deal with. Without such an understanding the utilitarian may criticize the retributive approach on the grounds that he

> ... sees nothing intrinsically fitting about this particular way, which itself involves increasing the misery in the world.[38]

But the infliction of the second-order suffering of punishment does not aim at increasing misery; rather, it presupposes an *existing* unhappy situation, and it is applied with the specific purpose of transforming this. Wrongdoing is not merely an act, but has repercussions on the personality of the wrongdoer; and in the absence of punishment, there is still first-order suffering for the wrongdoer. It is this factor which is neglected when, for instance, Bentham says:

> If we could consider an offence which has been committed as an isolated fact, the like of which would never recur, punishment would be useless.[39]

On our understanding, punishment would by no means be useless even in such an unlikely instance; the entail of the isolated offence would still need tackling. Here is another statement which is open to similar criticism:

> ... if the advantages of deterrence could be achieved by merely *seeming* to punish a criminal, would it not be *wrong* to do more than pretend to punish him, since the advantages could then be had without the disadvantages?[40]

Again, this misses the point that the criminal needs to be punished, i.e. a person who has committed wrong needs to be treated with an instrument that will tackle the consequences of wrongdoing in him. Not to punish is not to attempt to transform the consequences of wrongdoing. At this point utilitarian thought is in collusion with definitional retributivism, with its tendency to make guilt a necessary, but not sufficient, condition for punishment. On both sides there is insufficient understanding of the meaning and value of punishing the guilty.

In making these criticisms we do not wish to underestimate the positive value of utilitarian thought. It originated as a much-needed corrective to retributive abuses; and, when carefully and correctly interpreted, it stresses the importance of the humane treatment of offenders. It aims at the reformation, and indeed resocialization,[41] of the offender. It is only mistaken when it contrasts reformation with punishment, without realizing that punishment is itself the instrument for checking moral deterioration and promoting reformation. Without realizing, too, that if the concept of reformation is detached from that of desert, it becomes liable to sanction abuses, as already described. It is precisely on the basis of an integrated retributive view, and not otherwise, that the humane treatment of offenders becomes possible.

It has also been suggested that utilitarian thought is better able to take forgiveness into account:

It is one of the great embarrassments of the retributive theory that it is unable to give any consistent account of the duty of forgiveness and its relations to the duty of punishment.[42]

It is true that forgiveness is opposed to resentment and vengeance; but it is a serious mistake to equate these latter with a mature retributive understanding of punishment. Punishment is to be employed because wrongdoing has consequences for the wrongdoer, and the attempt to transform these consequences should not be seen as opposed to or incompatible with forgiveness. Whatever forgiveness is, it is not a desire to leave the wrongdoer subject to the entail of wrongdoing.

The position of punishment in the overall system of primary deterrence is another point that has been stressed by the utilitarians in particular. The punishment of the offender does help to deter other people, who might be potential offenders. But although this deterrence of other people is an important effect of punishment, it is not to be isolated from what punishment is in itself. To *threaten* punishment for crime if punishment is not in fact *inflicted* for crime, is nonsensical. If punishment is not inflicted *for* crime, if there really is no link between the two, why should the threat of punishment deter people *from* crime? Deterrence is neither meaningful nor effective unless it is based on retributive presuppositions. And it remains important to distinguish between secondary deterrence, of those who have not hitherto been deterred; and primary deterrence, of those who have so far been deterred. Punishment in itself aims at promoting secondary deterrence; granted this, one also sees that it has the wider effect of reinforcing the overall system of primary deterrence or crime prevention. But the two are not to be confused. Prevention may be better than cure, but when a crime has been committed one should not pretend that it has not been; and when a crime has not been committed, one may not act as if it has.

In sum, the chief contribution of the utilitarian approach to criminology has been its emphasis on the importance of the deterrence and reformation of the wrongdoer. We have suggested certain hazards to be found in uncritical utilitarianism: these will be obviated when utilitarian thought is reintegrated back into its proper, retributive matrix. To do this, we must reappropriate the meaning of punishment and of retribution. It is not correct to assert that

> the idea of 'reformation', which is concerned with the 'character' of man, is conceptually alien to the punitive scheme of criminal law.[43]

Concern for the wrongdoer's character and the need for his reformation is essential to the understanding of punishment we have here outlined. Likewise, we are unable to agree with the conclusion that

> ... social defence is largely based on the substitution of treatment for retributive punishment.[44]

Such an assertion, however benevolent in intention, has entirely missed the point of what punishment is about. Moreover, it is either otiose, if in fact 'treatment' proves to involve the same as does retributive punishment; or unjust, if it suggests that 'treatment' is to be imposed on someone who does not *deserve* it. But once the importance of desert is granted, we have taken our stand on an essentially retributive position. And as Bosanquet once pointed out,[45] if reformative theory and therapeutic treatment recognize and attempt to deal with the offender's bad will, there is nothing to distinguish this from other theories of punishment. Rightly so, for the offender's bad will—the effect of wrongdoing on his personality—is of central importance. Indeed, why should one wish to deter or reform anyone if this were not so? The innocent are not to be punished, because they do not have this bad will; the guilty are to be punished, because they do. One needs to take moral evil seriously. Any theory which did not do so would risk endangering the discernment of good and evil altogether. But it is only on the basis of such discernment that the vitally important concern for the wrongdoer's reformation and restoration to goodness can make any sense.

It will have become evident that what we are contending for is the recognition of the complementarity of the retributive and utilitarian approaches. In isolation or opposition each has notable limitations. But both are essential to the understanding of punishment. As we earlier expressed it, there are *two* drives underlying the theory of punishment, and both must be taken into account. But they may not be identified, either with each other or with punishment in itself. Thus, we need to enter the realm of moral being, and thence to reconstruct the meaning of punishment. This has been the approach of Sir Walter Moberly: a theory, one might say, of moral realism or of personal realism.

# 7

# The Suffering of the Guilty, Here and Hereafter

*Punishment ... gives expression and calls attention to a situation which is anyhow real.*[1]

It is a misleading oversimplification, but one all too often made, that punishment follows wrongdoing as one act following another act. This is true only in a superficial sense, and cannot serve to explain the significance of the given acts. The idea that punishment 'follows' wrongdoing must in any case be interpreted by our assertion that punishment is not itself a consequence of wrongdoing, even though subsequent to it. Apart from this caution, it is also important not to persist in interpreting guilty suffering solely in terms of acts of infliction—a prevalent, if not fully explicit, tendency. Wrongdoing is not merely an action, but the inauguration or reinforcement of a process of moral deterioration. What is *done* is symptomatic of and has repercussions on what one *is*. One may reiterate that the truest and most congruous retribution of wickedness is to lead a wicked life and become a wicked person. Likewise, punishment may in itself be an action—but this action has no meaning except with reference to the process of moral development which it is attempting to modify. To see either the *act* of wrongdoing alone, or the *act* of punishment alone, is to deprive oneself of the basis for understanding punishment. It is vital in addition to see the moral deterioration consequent on wrongdoing which it is hoped that punishment may modify. Otherwise one is left to observe two isolated, and strictly meaningless, actions.

However, precisely because the two 'orders' have repercussions on each other, our emphasis on moral being will not detract from the possibility of drawing practical conclusions from our discussion. Just as the actions of wrongdoing and of punishment are not to be isolated from their reference to what a person is becoming, so also what a person becomes affects what he does. It is the inner disposition which leads people to commit certain acts. Impenitence, or the unwillingness to repudiate the wrong one has done, may well lead one to commit further wrong or at any rate render one more prone to do so. Even when it does not do so, it will leave its mark on the personality to a greater or lesser degree, and to that extent is damaging. Penitence will involve relinquishing the state of mind that led one to commit wrong; one will seek to be good and to act as such. Thus, to speak of turning from impenitence to penitence is to talk in not merely theoretical terms, but with a direct practical bearing; even though instances of change will not always or even generally be as clear-cut as might be suggested by what is said here. Impenitence and penitence may be regarded as the two poles of a spectrum, or two broad categories from which individual instances will draw certain elements. The complexity of human nature is such that the pattern we are describing is to be taken as one to which individual change will in some degree approximate.

The distinction between the two 'orders' also helps us to understand the difference between the inevitable and the optional in guilty suffering. Punishment is optional, in the sense that it is an act imposed by decision. However, even if punishment were abolished, one could not do away with the first-order types of guilty suffering. These latter are intrinsically linked with wrongdoing. They are not a matter of infliction, and it is beyond human capacity to make them happen or not happen in a given person. One may decide to act or not to act, in imposing punishment, but penitence and impenitence are states of being, not actions. They cannot be imposed on a person directly. Indirectly, of course, they may be affected and this is precisely the purpose of punishment: to provide access to the first order, and to serve as an instrument for attempting to forestall continued impenitence and to promote penitence. To abolish punishment as second-order suffering is within human capacity but would indeed be shortsighted, for in this way one would abolish the very instrument which attempts to forestall the more serious first-order suffering —of moral deterioration—for which the wrongdoer is headed.

Fundamentally, the choice is not between imposing punishment and not imposing punishment, i.e. between imposing or not imposing some external constraint. It is between attempting to forestall continued moral deterioration—a process which the wrongdoer has inaugurated by his wrongful act—and not attempting to forestall this.

The wrongdoer has two options of guilty suffering, and he must choose one or other of these. There is no option which permits him to avoid guilty suffering in the first order altogether, since here—independently of punishment—guilty suffering is not optional, but inevitable. His only choice is as to which kind of suffering he will undergo. People may attempt to modify the guilty suffering that is a consequence of wrongdoing in the person of the wrongdoer, but ultimately, even with the intervention of the instrument of punishment, the choice lies with the wrongdoer himself, since the suffering that is moral deterioration is not something inflicted on the wrongdoer but is *his actual state*. The choice of suffering is but the choice of *being*, of what one wills to become—no more and no less than this.

The choice to continue in the state of mind which permitted one to commit wrong is not solely a choice to *act* in a certain way, though this too may be entailed. The whole personality is involved. One cannot *do* wrong without 'becoming wrong'. Moral deterioration is inevitable in the sense that one cannot do wrong and 'get away with it' in the moral sphere. However, it is not inevitable in the sense that it cannot in any way be forestalled. Evil can be repudiated, by penitence. But since moral deterioration is a condition inexorably attached to the commission of wrong, it cannot be avoided on terms that do less than justice to the full seriousness of wrong. Guilty suffering is inevitable when wrong has been committed—and not just inevitable, but in the strictest sense *proper*, in a universe which assumes the priority of the good.[2]

The alternative choice of suffering or moral being is that of penitence. This implies the repudiation of wrong and the return to goodness. The transformation of the consequences of wrongdoing in the wrongdoer is a moral change in the given personality. The transition from bad to good is necessarily an occasion of suffering in the realization of the true character of wrong, and of oneself as the wrongdoer, which is involved in one's realignment with the good. Sir Walter Moberly's study of punishment makes some reference to this type of guilty suffering. He says of the wrongdoer that

> ... punishment ... foreshadows the pain of conscience which must be his, if and when he comes to appreciate the meaning of his deed.[3]

Also,

> Pain or loss penally inflicted foreshadows 'the agony of returning animation', the pain of mind he will have to undergo if he is to recover ... penal pain must ultimately be transmuted into penitential pain.[4]

Penitence and moral deterioration are only similar in both being first-order forms of suffering. Otherwise, in their essential character they differ radically from each other, in that one is the prolongation of evil and the other is the restoration to goodness. In connection with this, it may be suggested that there is a notable difference in their subjective quality, i.e. in the way in which they are experienced by the persons concerned. The element of painfulness in penitence may be readily conceded. It is felt in the willingness to see wrong in the light of goodness. But continuation in the state of wrong would seem to be characterized by a growing *in*sensitivity or 'hardness of heart'. It may be seen as the development of moral anaesthesia, dangerous precisely because of its diminishing ability to feel the pain of the contrast between good and evil.[5] It is termed suffering in that it involves deterioration of the personality, and in that it is contrary to personal life and the happiness that is an intrinsic quality of goodness. Thus too, although one may speak of the suffering of moral deterioration as an evil, the suffering that is penitence—even if painful—ought not to be called an *evil*. It is suffering, moral suffering, but it is certainly not a matter of moral evil. Of the two options of moral suffering, one is undoubtedly evil, but the other is undoubtedly good.

Just because these types of guilty suffering are in essence states of being—understood dynamically, as what the wrongdoer is becoming in the course of personal growth—it is in fact pointless to seek the cessation of either as a phenomenon. The suffering of penitence ceases when penitence has reached its fulfilment, in restoration to the good. Short of this, one may remain in a state of relative impenitence. One can only 'avoid' the suffering of penitence if one chooses to fall short of restoration. There is no alternative route to the goal of restoration. The suffering that is penitence *is* the transition from wrong to goodness, not an independent phenomenon, and to stop the suffering short of fulfilling its function is to stop the process of transition short of reaching its goal.

Moral deterioration is likewise a state of being or becoming, and hence one cannot seek the cessation of it as a phenomenon of *suffering* except by forestalling the state of *being* that it actually is. In other words, one cannot remain hardened in wrong without suffering its effects. If one wishes not to suffer in this way one must take a decision not to continue in hardness of heart. But one cannot be impenitent, i.e. remain in a state of wrong, and at the same time avoid the suffering of moral deterioration, simply inasmuch as these are one and the same thing. The kinds of suffering that are of the first order cannot cease as phenomena without being worked through on ethical terms. The voluntary element in guilty suffering is the choice of the wrongdoer to be penitent or to remain impenitent; one cannot just choose 'not to suffer'.

The moral consequences of wrongdoing may be worked through, by penitence, as soon as the wrongdoer so chooses. But the state of impenitence may continue indefinitely, and in any case is a cumulative process of moral deterioration—it is not asserted that complete deterioration follows immediately on any one act of wrongdoing. The wrongdoer might perhaps be spoken of as one who is *not yet* penitent, though one may not assert that anything can ever *compel* him to be penitent; and certainly the consequences of wrongdoing are not yet fully worked through, short of the moral decision that is involved in the transition back to goodness. Penitence is not limited by a time-factor, in the sense that no given length of time *need* elapse before penitence occurs, though in any given instance penitence may take place after some length of time. Impenitence, on the other hand, may last indefinitely, though it need not do so; its duration is a matter for the wrongdoer's own decision. In the last resort, nobody can make the decision for him against his will, even though others may hope to influence his decision. But length of duration in impenitence is in no way conducive to the resolution of the situation, but marks its continuing lack of resolution. Consequences cannot 'run to exhaustion', however long impenitence lasts. This is because the moral deterioration that it implies is the intrinsic outworking of the act of wrongdoing—the continuation of the state of wrong. It is not and cannot be the resolution which is restoration to the good.

Wrongdoing, which marked a break in the true functioning of interdependence, may be continued and consummated in complete deterioration and the final breakdown of interdependence. The choice of wrong is incompatible with being in a state of right-relatedness. If the decision for wrong is perpetuated, so likewise is the deterioration in relatedness. By contrast, penitence is not just a return to goodness, understood in the abstract, but to the right-relatedness which was disrupted by the original wrongdoing. Penitence is in this way to be seen within the context of reconciliation.

Both penitence and impenitence are seen to be integrally linked with a person's state of being, with what he is becoming for good or for ill. Because of this, one may speak of guilty suffering in both immediate and ultimate terms, since the two options themselves point to man's ultimate becoming. Hence it will be of value to reassess the traditional Christian concepts of the afterlife on this basis.

Broadly speaking, the overall concept of the afterlife is subdivided into either two or three distinct ideas: heaven and hell; or heaven, purgatory, and hell. Perhaps popular contemporary thought goes even further than this and would speak only of heaven, thus concluding the diminution of options which has characterized western Christian thought since medieval times: first, three options; then (for Reformed thought) only two options; and now, finally, one option. Our purpose here will be to reassess the ideas of hell and purgatory, on the grounds that their uncritical rejection is hardly more justified than what was perhaps their previously uncritical acceptance.

First, though, it will be useful to remind ourselves of some of the reasons for the increasing unacceptability of these options. To a large extent the essence of the ideas which these options have attempted to express has been overlaid by a variety of inessential accretions. In particular, the pictorial imagery attached to the concepts of hell and purgatory has become increasingly difficult to accept, especially when literal acceptance has been pressed for. Such imagery has by now largely lost whatever value or validity it may be deemed to have possessed.

However, it has not just been a question of unacceptable imagery as such. Two more important points underlie this. First, it would seem that much of such imagery should be ascribed to illegitimate speculation. How far can one genuinely build up a picture of the afterlife, and on what basis may one do so? Second, what is implied by such ideas for our understanding of the character of God and of man and of their mutual relationship? On this second count it becomes clear that a major factor in the rejection of the ideas of purgatory and hell has been their apparent incongruity with the revealed and known character of God and of his dealings with man. If God is love, if Christ lived and died and rose again for love of us, then one will not accept an idea of God or of his action that is contrary to this. In practice this will lead to the rightful rejection of any idea of the afterlife which presents God as, say, a vindictive torturer. This is not to divorce love from ethical concern. Love is not to be confused with sentimentality, and the implication for us of the statement that God is love *is* an overwhelming ethical concern, taking fully seriously the human situation of good and evil. Hell is not rendered unacceptable for reasons of mere sentiment. But, precisely because of the ethical seriousness of love, one may with reasonable confidence of accuracy point to what is radically incompatible with this assertion.

What is the essence of the ideas of purgatory and hell, and is this rendered unacceptable along with the traditional imagery? One may note in passing that the diversity of imagery has not so radically devalued the concept of heaven, since—perhaps through an instinctive sense of priorities—the imagery has been allowed to aid and not to supplant what is essential to the concept. I would venture to suggest that the preceding discussion of guilty suffering may serve as a kind of critical apparatus for the reassessment of the concepts of purgatory and hell. We will not go beyond what has already been asserted but simply reapply the given framework. This is not to make the theological doctrines of hell and purgatory *dependent* on experiences in the moral order, but is an attempt to find the most helpful means of giving *content* to these doctrines.

One assumption is being made in this discussion, and that is that there is an afterlife. I do not intend to argue the case for or against this (which might in any case be somewhat inconclusive), but will take it as a generally accepted presupposition of Christian theology and explore its implications. It has already been indicated that Christian thought understands by this more than solely subsequent temporality.[6] It does not exclude all notions of chronology, but is qualitative as well as chronological. There is not only subsequent eschatology, but also inaugurated eschatology.[7] Inaugurated eschatology does not preclude subsequent eschatology, but what has been inaugurated may be said to have subsumed to itself all the possible categories of what is subsequent, i.e. what is subsequent may not be contrary to what has already begun.

The assessment of concepts of the afterlife, understood as subsequent eschatology, will benefit from the consideration of realized eschatology, in that it provides a basis for discussion that is not merely speculative. This is of importance for the question already raised in connection with the afterlife: what do such concepts assert about the nature of God and of man and of their mutual relation? Negatively, we have said that such concepts must be criticized, and if necessary dismissed, if shown to be incompatible with the known character of God's dealings with man. Positively—to reshape this latter statement—it may be said that what is known, particularly in and through Christ incarnate, to be God's way of acting vis-à-vis mankind gives us a most certain criterion and confidence for the understanding of 'what will ultimately be', in principle, if not in detail. God will not be untrue to himself, and nothing can be true of the afterlife that is false to what is known in this life. What is true of God and man here and now will not be contradicted.

We have seen how penitence and impenitence are intimately linked with what a person actually *becomes*, both immediately and—more significantly for this discussion—in ultimate terms. In effect, these two options may be seen to correspond with the given concepts of the afterlife. Penitence corresponds with the idea of purgatory; and impenitence culminating in intransigence would correspond with the idea of hell. Both purgatory and hell involve the suffering of the guilty. Hell, just as intransigence, speaks of the prolongation of the state of wrong and the suffering of its effects. And purgatory, just as penitence, speaks of the move from wrong towards goodness and the suffering involved in this move. In describing penitence and intransigence, we may equally speak of purgatory and hell respectively. Or rather, what may be said about penitence and intransigence is not to be limited in its application to the conditions of life here and now. If it is valid at all, it may be hypothesized that it applies equally both now and hereafter. Our understanding of the concepts of purgatory and hell is thus not imaginative but rather a corollary implicit in the given understanding of guilty suffering.

One may speak not only of penitence and impenitence as subsequent to this life; but also, perhaps, of purgatory and hell as having some reality in this life, as inaugurated eschatology and not just as subsequent eschatology. Purgatory certainly may and has been spoken of in terms of this life, the classic example of this being St John of the Cross' exposition of the Dark Night of the Soul. However, although there may be an increasing process of moral deterioration within this life, the term 'hell' should probably be reserved for the completion of this process—if it is completed. This differing use of the two terms vis-à-vis the present life would seem to correspond to what has been said about the time-factor in guilty suffering. The process of penitence may take place as soon as it is desired—'desired' in the sense of choosing to make a moral decision for it. But the process of impenitence and moral deterioration has no specified termination short of the decision for a change of heart. Thus, penitence or the purgatorial process may be opted for without delay, here and now as well as there and then. But impenitence may continue indefinitely; and short of its irrevocable consummation it is the state of one who is not yet penitent, but may yet be so.

Some interesting corollaries emerge from the interpretation of purgatory and hell in terms of the given pattern of guilty suffering. Penitence and impenitence are the two options open to the wrongdoer. The choice is only between these two, i.e. there are no other options, and no possibility of avoiding these particular options. Nor are there less than two options. As regards the afterlife this is to assert the propriety of *both* purgatory and hell, as the two options of guilty suffering. One without the other in the afterlife would be as meaningless as one without the other in the given discussion of guilty suffering. There is something to turn from—moral deterioration; and something to turn to—the restoration to goodness. Neither of these two may be left out of sight without making nonsense of the remaining option. Still less is there any justification for dismissing both altogether.

One-option theories, of whatever sort, must be considered inadequate. To speak of hell without mentioning purgatory is to speak of intransigence without the possibility of penitence, which is deterministic. True, hell or ultimate moral deterioration cannot be forestalled by merely wishing it, but it can be forestalled by a moral decision of turning from it. It may at this point be objected that to speak of hell without mentioning purgatory is not to speak of one option alone, in that hell may be contrasted with heaven. But the two-option scheme is one of guilty suffering, and so in this way heaven may not be 'paired off' with hell. Even if considered as subsequent to purgatory, heaven is not (any longer) a matter of guilty suffering. Heaven may be contrasted with the possibility of hell only in the discussion of 'final states'. Prior to final realization the choice is between two options of guilty suffering. In any case there is no possibility of leaping straight from intransigence (and hell) to the fully restored state of goodness (and heaven) *except* by the moral decision of turning from the bad and to the good which is penitence. Purgatory is the very *definition* of the transfer from the one to the other. Perhaps it is because penitence (and purgatory) are not comparable in duration to impenitence that there has been at times a tendency to focus on the one—which may last indefinitely, short of a moral decision to turn from it; and to minimize or 'telescope' the other—which will cease as soon as its purpose is achieved, and hence is not of indefinite duration. But this is not to excuse neglect of the second option: impenitence may not be spoken of without acknowledging the possibility of penitence as well.

Universalism likewise suffers from the deficiencies of a one-option scheme. It may be regarded as a kind of attenuated doctrine of purgatory, but taken in isolation as one option alone. It does not necessarily demand immediacy of realization, but usually states that all will get to heaven 'in the end'. In thus allowing for a delay before ultimate realization, universalism is comparable to the process aspect of purgatory. It does not, however, do justice to the essentially penitential character of the process of guilty suffering that is purgatory, and in this respect it is a somewhat colourless doctrine. Moreover, universalism does not make any allowance for the possibility of hell, the other option. It is not that this latter option *has* to be realized, but that there is a definite and necessary possibility of it, which requires to be acknowledged. Universalism, as a one-option scheme, does not take fully seriously the implications of evil. It is as if one were to say that people must be, and can only be, penitent. But, although people may choose to turn from the will to wrong, one cannot determine or compel the choice. To state that all will be saved, where 'will' equals 'must', is to postulate a kind of determinism. This determinism in itself constitutes a fundamental objection, but there is in any case a failure to do justice to the definition of penitence and the restoration to goodness. One has to turn *to* these, *from* wrong and its concomitant moral deterioration: a prior state of wrong is presupposed by the definition of penitence. In sum, one-option schemes are seen to be invalid. One cannot hope to do justice to the data without interpreting them in terms of the two options of guilty suffering. To speak of both penitence and impenitence leads one to speak of both purgatory and hell.

Historically, there has been the tendency to focus on one or other option in isolation. The Reformation led to the abandonment of the idea of purgatory by a large sector of Christendom, instead of a reassessment and refinement of what might be true in the idea. Hell was 'paired off' with heaven, and in consequence immediacy and irrevocability of one's ultimate destiny was insisted on. No longer was the purgatorial *process* matched against the *process* of moral deterioration. The definition of impenitence was narrowed to that of ultimate intransigence alone, without the concept of an indefinitely enduring state of impenitence. The precious possibility of seeing impenitence as the state of one who is not *yet* penitent was lost sight of, and the possibility of change gave way to a demand for immediacy of final realization.

This is not to imply that the acceptance of both purgatory and hell necessitates the acceptance of any specific length of time or duration before the realization of one's ultimate destiny. To postulate this would be unwarranted. But one may, conversely, state that they imply that death ought not of itself to be taken to imply finality and irrevocability of destiny. Death may be the transition to the *after*life, but it is not—arguably—the *beginning* of eschatological realization. To allow death such a position would be to lose all sense of inaugurated eschatology—the Christian insight that eschatological realization may begin here and now, in this life. To interpret eschatology solely in terms of subsequent temporality, i.e. only after death, would not seem to do justice to the Christian understanding in its fullness. Conversely, to see death as the finally decisive turning-point for moral growth and for the fulfilment or otherwise of one's relationship with God, would seem to be inconsistent with what is known of personality. If moral growth cannot of its very nature be forced, it seems *unlikely*—certainly somewhat incongruous—that there could be an abrupt consummation of personal development. One cannot be dogmatic about this, but it would seem more likely that growth and deterioration are possible both in this life and hereafter: neither one's present relationship with God, nor the present lack of such a relationship, *have* to preclude the possibility of personal growth and change and development.

The demand for the immediate realization of one's ultimate destiny after death has not, it would seem, been consistently made by those who neglect to have a specific doctrine of purgatory. The idea of there being something before the consummation of one's destiny, and yet after death, is to be found in the concept of the Last Judgement. Although not itself descriptive of a process of becoming, it does in some sense allow for an 'interval'—in the given sense of being subsequent to death and prior, if only immediately prior, to the fulfilment of one's destiny. This, in addition, is the only way in which one can reasonably answer the question of *when* the Last Judgement is supposed to take place—one may not safely specify more than this.

In what terms are we to think of such a judgement? Judgement here and now is something external to the personality, just as punishment is something external. But punishment points beyond itself to guilty suffering in the first order, and it is in terms of first-order suffering that we are analysing concepts of the afterlife, as what is true and ultimately true of moral being. Thus, just as first-order suffering is a matter of what one is becoming—one suffers by virtue of what one is, by virtue of one's moral state—it would seem that judgement in turn is to be viewed as *the statement of what we have become and are*. It is no longer something imposed *ab extra* or a partial critique of one's actions. Rather it is an intrinsic judgement, a complete critique of all that one is. What one has *done* is but symptomatic of what one has *become*.

Such an understanding of the Last Judgement, as the final statement of what we have become, might well presuppose a process of becoming, and this would suggest that the idea is more compatible with schemes that do not demand immediate realization of one's ultimate destiny. The Last Judgement would seem to be the consummation of the process of growth, not its abrogation. It is by definition something final; but at the same time it is the fulfilment of what has gone before.

The realization of eschatology—though not completed and consummated—has begun, and hence we must also consider what is happening in the present life. The Last Judgement may be the final statement of what we have become, but here and now we are moral beings making moral choices, the very choices that will 'one day' form the substance of this final declaration. Our immediate choices, of penitence or impenitence, are morally significant and carry their own judgement with them, of what we are becoming for good or for ill.

We shall now examine more closely each of the two options. First, the idea of hell. The possibility of hell is not a piece of isolated speculation, but a corollary of the nature of wrong. It may be of use to spell this out. Moral deterioration is the outworking of the state of wrong, and is fully congruous with it. The two are very strictly commensurable. Hell would be the consummation of the state of wrong, the finalization of the intrinsic outworking of wrongdoing. It is the condition attached (ultimately) to unrepudiated wrongdoing—not an arbitrary condition, but the statement of what unrepudiated wrongdoing of its very nature entails and *is*. It would be the ultimate statement of what a person had become in terms of evil. Thus, a person could not be 'condemned' to hell as something external to himself; he would be 'in' hell by reason of what he would *be*, what he himself had chosen to become. The possibility of hell is a necessary possibility simply in that evil is evil. Sin is a self-destructive force. A person could not be 'out of' hell without choosing to turn from wrong. Continuation in the state of wrong would preclude one from heaven since it is *of its own nature* incompatible with it. Ultimately, wrong does coincide with misery, and goodness with happiness, in that they are inherently related and not fundamentally anything external to each other. If the hell of ultimate intransigence is one of moral deterioration and the breakdown of interdependence, then the bliss of goodness and interdependence cannot be attained except on condition of moral change: the renunciation of the choice for what is intrinsically incompatible with these, and making the decision for penitence and the restoration to goodness. It is only the decision to cling to wrong that may make one 'fit for hell'. To have committed wrong, *and to have repented of it*, is no barrier but rather the removal of barriers. Heaven is peopled not by the innocent, but by the redeemed.

It has been the neglect of the distinction between the possible and the actual that has led to so much confusion in the traditional discussion of hell. The possibility of hell has been confused with the actualization of the possibility, and there has been a failure to appreciate that, although the possibility is necessary, its actualization is not. Confusion of the two has led to the assertion either that the possibility *must* be actualized, which asserts too much; or that there cannot even be the possibility, which asserts too little and does not do justice to what is meant by moral evil.

Since it is important to recognize the conditional nature of hell, it may be better to speak of what it 'would be' rather than of what it 'is' or 'will be'. It *is* a condition attached to continuance in the state of wrong, but it is *only* a condition and need not be realized. One cannot compel a person to turn from wrong, but neither can one compel him not to make this decision. To see impenitence as the state of someone who is not yet penitent reflects the conditionality of the outworking of wrongdoing, which in turn ultimately reflects the priority of good in the universe. Because of this priority of the good, evil—though fully real, in the sense of not being illusory—can only be regarded as conditional, and as something the continuation of which it is considered proper to forestall (unlike continuation in the state of good, which one certainly does not feel obliged to forestall!). A wrongful disposition may at some point be checked by a moral decision of turning from it. Moral deterioration can be forestalled, and can only be forestalled, on these terms.

Is it possible, though, that there might be unending

intransigence? For the state to be indefinitely prolonged is not necessarily for it to last unendingly. However, this would seem to be *possible*, and all that we may do is to reiterate that the possibility need not be realized and to hope that it will not be. We are not entitled to say that it cannot be. On the other hand, it is not for us to state at what point unrepudiated wrongdoing is irrevocably unrepudiated. *We* cannot specify the 'point of no return'. The conditional nature of the state of wrong implies no determinism, of either sort. One may not say that a given person either must remain in wrong and 'be damned', or must turn from wrong and 'be saved'. Each of these statements would be the expression of a one-option scheme—of hell without the possibility of penitence, or of some form of universalism. For the reasons already given, one-option schemes must be regarded as untenable. The fact that there is truly an option of enduring impenitence, and thus of the *possibility* of hell, must be taken into account. However, we must equally bear in mind the fact that it is but one of two options, and that it is only conditional. This gives us genuine grounds for hope. The *termination* of intransigence is not its *consummation*. We are not entitled to speculate as to the actual finalization of intransigence, but we may and should note that its termination, its only specified termination, is the decision to turn from impenitence to penitence.

It is also of considerable importance to note that the possibility of hell is not to be confused with the traditional idea of 'eternal punishment'. Continuation in intransigence, even perhaps the consummation of intransigence (whatever that might be), is in no sense eternal *punishment*. To suggest this is a serious abuse of the word 'punishment'. Punishment is in itself external, of the second order; it is instrumental and intermediate, not itself something final. Above all, it is referential, and symbolic of what is happening in the first order. It is not to be confused with either of its referents. Yet this is precisely the mistake that is made when hell is equated with 'eternal punishment': *it is the confusion of punishment with moral deterioration*, which is but one of its referents and quite distinct from punishment. The hell that is moral deterioration is not to be equated with the very instrument that would attempt to forestall it! Spelled out in this way, one sees the absurdity of the traditional idea. However, it was perfectly possible for such confusion to arise so long as the general theory of punishment was similarly confused and the nature of punishment not clearly elucidated. It is only the symbolic theory of punishment that at last provides one with a satisfactory critique for the idea of 'eternal punishment'.

Surprisingly enough, Sir Walter Moberly did not himself work out this corollary of his main theory, and his discussion[8] of the idea of eternal punishment does not make use of the excellent critical instrument that his theory would have provided. But to some extent, despite this signal disadvantage, he still tends towards the sort of conclusions we have suggested. He says, for instance:

> The whole process of sin is a progressive alienation from God; and the climax of such a progressive alienation is that essential incompatibleness with God which we call Hell.[9]

Again:

> Such a condition does not merely deserve or entail, it itself *is*, eternal death.[10]

And, most importantly:

> The ultimate issue is not between destruction and salvation (understood as torment suffered or as infinite happiness), it is between sin and holiness themselves . . .[11]

On this note we shall turn to the idea of purgatory. In contrast to impenitence, penitence is not of indefinite duration but finds its termination *and* consummation in its goal of restoration, whereas the termination of impenitence is the *forestalling* of its consummation. Purgatory could not be its own termination, for its 'finalization' is heaven. Purgatory is essentially a process, of our growth from the bad to the good. One sees sin and one's own sinfulness in the light of God; and it is this realism of self-knowledge that is of the essence of the suffering involved in penitence. Because it is a process of what one is actually becoming, one is judged not just for one's acts, as distinct from oneself, but for all that one *is and has been*. The judgement is the suffering, and judgement and suffering alike are no more and no less than the statement of what one is. It is the realization of the contrast between sin (oneself the sinner) and goodness, and hence the intense longing for restoration, that account for this form of suffering. In the words of the classic account of St Catherine of Genoa: 'The more it sees, the more extreme is its pain.'[12] St Catherine also uses the traditional metaphor of 'fire' to describe this:

> Sin's rust is the hindrance, and the fire burns the rust away so that more and more the soul opens itself up to the divine inflowing.[13]

This 'fire' is understood as the love of God, the burning effect of which is felt only to the extent to which sin still has a hold in one, before one has come to the realization of the fullness of self-knowledge in the light of the knowledge of God. Ultimately this 'fire' will no longer 'burn'. It will be not burning, but bliss.

> (The purified soul) . . . can suffer no more, for nothing is left in it, to be burned away; were it held in the fire when it has thus been cleansed, it would feel no pain. Rather, the fire of divine love would be to it like eternal life and in no way contrary to it.[14]

Within western Christendom the possibility of purgatory has sometimes been disputed on the grounds that no penitential process is possible subsequent to death. The understanding of the afterlife is telescoped into a demand for the immediate realization of one's ultimate destiny. This is an idea that we have already criticized. Moreover, although the primary moment of penitence for the Christian may be the entry to the Christian life (conversion, baptism), it is nevertheless very largely understood that there will be moments of penitence subsequent to this. And if one allows for penitence subsequent to entry into the Christian life, one has in effect granted the principle necessary for belief in purgatory, which is but the (ultimate) outworking of penitence, and which in any case may begin in this life.

In looking at various aspects of penitence, there is one problem that we have reserved for special consideration: the sheer difficulty of penitence, owing to weakness of will. The problem is well stated by R. C. Moberly in his discussion of penitence:

> Penitence, on analysis, is found to require no less than personal identification with absolute holiness; but with holiness particularly in its aspect as the absolute condemnation of sin.[15]

Penitence involves the alignment of the whole personality with righteousness; it is 'perfect will-identity with God in condemnation of sin'.[16] In the transformation of the penitent, the personality which had identified itself with the 'will of sin' is re-identified with righteousness in its opposition to sin.[17] The consummation of penitence would thus involve 'a real personal self-identity with the consciousness of sin ... as seen by God'.[18]

However, all penitence within our experience is imperfect. What it can do is to indicate the nature of penitence, and within its limitations it is genuinely restorative.[19] But there still remains the problem of how it may be fully achieved within human personality. Undoubtedly the more one has sinned the greater is one's need of repentance, but for this same reason repentance is all the more difficult.

> The reality of sin in the self blunts the self's power of utter antithesis against sin ... The more I have been habituated to sinning, the feebler is my capacity of contrition. But even once to have sinned is to have lost once for all its ideal perfectness. It is sin, as sin, which blunts the edge, and dims the power, of penitence.[20]

Sin has marred the very capacity for repentance. One is no longer able to discern the 'sinfulness of sin', and one's identification with sin detracts from the possibility of identification with righteousness. The least real affinity of the self with sin 'impairs the possibility of that perfect self-identity with righteousness which is necessary for the consummation of perfect penitence'.[21] This leads to the paradoxical conclusion that

> penitence is absolutely necessary for us in proportion as it is impossible, and impossible in proportion as it is necessary ...[22] A true penitence is as much the inherent impossibility, as it is the inherent necessity, of every man that has sinned.[23]

Thus stated, we are faced with a dilemma—but it may be resolved. What is difficult for us by ourselves becomes readily capable of realization through the indwelling of the Holy Spirit, the Spirit of Pentecost. It is this that is 'the reality of the penitence of the really penitent'.[24]

For what is the real consummation of the atonement to be? It is to be the very Spirit of the Crucified become our spirit—

ourselves translated into the Spirit of the Crucified. The Spirit of the Crucified, the Spirit of Him who died and is alive, may be, and please God shall be, the very constituting reality of ourselves.[25]

In this way the reality of the penitence which is part of normal Christian experience is itself the guarantee of the consummation of our penitence, for it is the life of the Holy Spirit within us, through whom we live in Christ and he in us. It is Christ himself who is our 'capacity of responsive holiness'.[26] Indeed 'it is only through Pentecost that the meaning of human personality is ever actually realized at all'.[27] It is the Christian life that brings to fulfilment what we have said about penitence and restoration.

This conclusion that we have reached is of considerable importance as regards both the content and, no less, the method of theology. In effect, it marks the transition between the two theological methods used in this study. We have been discussing guilty suffering. This is theologically significant in two ways. First, in that it is morally significant, i.e. even without explicit reference to the theology of redemption, for moral being may be understood as part of the content of natural theology. Second, it provides a frame of reference for the understanding of the Christian life. The acceptance of a relationship with Christ is to turn us from the will to wrong ('Christ came to save the lost') and to receive us, through penitence, to restoration ('repent, and be saved'). The question of man underlying the atonement is one of how the sinful may be 'saved' from their state; that something has gone wrong with man and needs to be righted; that man is to be brought from breakdown in relatedness to right-relatedness with God and with man in God. In this one is not 'invoking Christ' in order to back up a humanistic scheme of understanding. Just as Christ became fully human, so he came to fulfil all that is fully human and to enable us to fulfil the purpose for which we were created. Man was created in the image of God, and the fulfilment of humanity is the fulfilment of God's purpose for humanity. (It is the state of sin and wrong that is less than human, in the most proper and normative sense of the word.) Hence, we may fittingly speak of some aspects of the atonement and of its outworking in terms of human life, of the human state as it is and as it should be. In this we have made extensive use of the language of the theology of creation, or natural theology. The aim in so doing has been to shed light on something of what the atonement presupposes, understood as the restoration of creation to the purposes of its creator. However, the same material may and should also be transposed into the specific language of the theology of redemption, and this is what our consideration of R. C. Moberly on penitence has led us to do. We have considered moral being as such: by a process of translation we come to consider it within the specific framework of the Christian life.

# 8

# The Theology of Penitence: A Study of the Christian Life

Penitence is definitive of entering into relationship with Christ. At the same time, to say that penitence may be more than just a statement of moral experience is not to repudiate our preceding analysis of it. Indeed, the idea of 'turning' is incorporated into theological vocabulary in the word 'conversion'.[1] One turns from impenitence to penitence; from moral deterioration to the restoration to goodness; to a relationship with Christ from a state that was not this. In talking of conversion, it is still true to say that it presupposes two states of being, one of which is to be forestalled and the other to be promoted. Thus, the twofold movement of turning is basic to the experience of becoming a Christian. The aspect of turning *from* something, as the necessary initial step in this twofold movement, may be taken up by a variety of ministries at the point of entry to the Christian life. Three of these may be mentioned.

First, exorcism. Although exorcism may be used on a variety of occasions, and for Christians and non-Christians alike, one of its most normative uses is at the point of entry to the Christian life, immediately preceding the baptismal service.[2] Entry into relationship with Christ implies both turning from, and deliverance from, sin or 'the powers of evil' or life that is outside of and contrary to relationship with Christ. The service of exorcism indicates with particular clarity that the personal choice of the candidate, to turn from what is wrong, must be supplemented by something beyond the given person, i.e. by the ministry of deliverance. A common mistake is to interpret exorcism too narrowly or to link it with unacceptable imagery. The reality of evil is not to be reduced to such imagery, and hence it is not to be dismissed along with it. Exorcism is not something isolated but is one particular focus of a much wider ministry, in that deliverance is a key concept in the outworking of the atonement and hence is a major theme of the Christian life. Exorcism is not of course the whole of this ministry, but it is an integral part of it. The deliverance of the atonement cannot be restricted to *sin* alone, as perhaps there has been a tendency to do in contemporary thought, but refers to the whole range of *evil*, of which the sinful constitutes some large part. Thus, exorcism does have a part to play in the deliverance and healing and reintegration that accompanies and brings to realization the reorientation of a person that is conversion.

Such healing is not confined to exorcism. There may be a need for the 'healing of memories' which, as a specific ministry, has been brought into prominence largely through the charismatic movement. It is important to be able to face all of the past, for it to be cleansed and healed. In psychological terms this ministry involves a kind of abreaction. Memories that have been repressed or forgotten or in any way distorted are brought to the conscious mind to be faced and dealt with, and so will no longer constitute a threat to psychological or spiritual health. The healing of memories will also be an ongoing process throughout the Christian life. In particular, it is part of what is sometimes known as the 'Dark Night of the Soul'. It should in any case be seen as a normal development of man's relationship with God.

A large and particularly important aspect of deliverance is to be seen in terms of yet another category: that of penance, which involves the personal acknowledgement and repudiation of personal wrong. This is not to suggest that the penitent's own desire or decision is the only thing that counts, though. Forgiveness is vital, and absolution is itself an act of healing. The sacrament of penance may also be understood as a sacrament of reconciliation, and in this sense it may be seen as a kind of renewal of baptism. The entry into the Christian life is a personal act, but not the act of an isolated individual. It has a corporate dimension, of entering into relation with all others who are in relation to Christ. It is a movement into a deeper level of interdependence. The sacrament of penance is a reaffirmation of this, by further healing anything that detracts from the proper functioning of interdependence. Penitence is not to be isolated from restoration and reconciliation.

The ministry of healing and deliverance will in this way take on a variety of forms. Concretely, this will involve many areas of life: the reorientation and healing of one's priorities, one's relationships, one's time and timetable. To turn to God in conversion is not to be reduced to an abstract generalization, and the offering of oneself to God must involve all the particularities of everyday life, if it is not to be unreal. Conversion should involve all that one is and has been. Everything is to be opened up and offered to God, the good as well as the bad. The bad is to be healed, and delivered from, and forgiven. And all else is to be placed at God's disposal and so to be set free from self-centredness.

The movement of conversion is not to be linked solely with the moment of *entering* into relationship with Christ. Conversion, as turning (from sin) to Christ, is definitive of the entire Christian life. To speak of a life of conversion is not to deny a (first) moment of conversion but rather to confirm it. Historically, baptism was at first seen as the decisive moment of repentance—the only such moment—and originally no place was allowed for subsequent repentance. This may have been intended to underline the importance of baptism, but in effect seriously limited the understanding of its value. Baptism was regarded as a guarantee of faultlessness, rather than as the mark of an abiding possibility of repentance and restoration. In course of time this latter view prevailed, and it came to be seen that just because the entry into the Christian life is a decisive moment of repentance and conversion, it must be possible for this to be continued and renewed, as the outworking of the initial moment and proof of its decisiveness.

The idea that there is something subsequent to the first moment of conversion, or to baptism, may be expressed in various ways. The underlying principle is one of continuing growth, to Christian maturity. In view of this there may be the call for 'sanctification' or 'complete holiness' subsequent to 'justification'. The charismatic movement would speak of 'baptism in the Spirit' for someone who is already a Christian. The monastic life is sometimes spoken of as an intensification of the baptismal life, or the outworking of the Christian life generally may be described as the 'manifestation of baptism'.[3] And in the Eucharist above all there is the reaffirmation and deepening of our life in Christ. Most sectors of Christendom would in some form or other recognize the principle of growth subsequent to entry to the Christian life.

The whole of one's life is involved in conversion. It cannot ultimately be less than a turning of the whole person to Christ, the offering of all of oneself. It is also the matter of a lifetime. The monastic ideal, of the whole of life as conversion, is true of the Christian life generally. Our life is to be one of a continual turning to God, our growth as persons is a matter of our growth in relationship with Christ. 'The truly matured man is the completely converted man.'[4]

Conversion understood as reorientation is something that most specifically develops in terms of prayer. This is not particularly a question of 'having a spiritual life', as one part of something larger, but is a matter of living all of one's life in relation to God. It will focus on specific times devoted exclusively to prayer, but the underlying aim will be one of learning to *be* prayer and not just to *do* prayer, as one thing among other things. In the Orthodox tradition this aim is expressed as 'standing constantly before God, with the mind in the heart', i.e. with all one's being.[5] Primarily it will be a matter of relationship—one's relationship with Christ—rather than a matter of technique, except insofar as techniques of training in prayer are helpful in enabling one to be attentive and responsive in the given relationship. Learning to pray is important, not as the performance of a religious exercise, but as a matter of growth in relationship. In this growth in relationship, which for us *is* our conversion or reorientation to God, attentiveness is one of the basic things to be learned. This is to be done in specific times of prayer in such a way that it becomes a basic disposition in everything, an abiding orientation. It should arise quite simply and realistically from the recognition that there are *two* sides to a relationship, that there is Someone to Whom we can and should be attentive. In practice, it may begin by the refusal to let prayer be a monologue—by not speaking all through one's prayer-time, and by letting the 'gaps' be governed by an intention of attentiveness. From this kind of basis other levels of silence in prayer may be learned. One's own task is to be prepared and responsive for whatever God chooses to give or not to give, in the freedom of a genuine relationship.

Moral and spiritual experience alike are to be linked with personal growth. We find that here again the emphasis is on what one *is*, rather than on what one *does*. Goodness as well as evil is a state of being that issues in acts, not just the acts taken in isolation from the state of the person who commits them. It is important to bear this in mind when we attempt to speak theologically of goodness.

How, in the process of penitence and conversion, does *doing* good relate to *being* good? What is God's part (grace) and what is man's part (freewill)? What is the proper relation of 'faith' and 'works'?

The idea that one is 'justified' by grace through faith, rather than by 'works', is an assertion of the priority of being over doing—that what one is is of greater importance than what one does. At the same time, and most importantly, this involves the repudiation of autonomy. There is always the temptation with good deeds to regard them as one's own, in a self-assertive sense. But the process of 'becoming for good' or conversion is not something autonomous, it is turning to God and growth in relationship with him. Any actions stemming from this relationship are unambiguously good by reason of what they express. Outside of this relationship good actions are ambivalent. In particular they may be the expression of an attempt at self-justification, which is to miss the point that it is *only* the relationship with God, or lack of it, which is ultimately important. It is not that good deeds are to be regarded as wrongful, but that they are in a fundamental sense irrelevant. Doing is only significant as an expression of being; and, when deeds as such can be ambivalent, it is all the more important to keep this sense of priorities. Do any given good deeds stem from a relationship with God, or do they represent an attempt to secure one's salvation independently of the relationship which *is* salvation?

One sees the development of this ambivalence in the history of the nation Israel's relation with God. At first Israel is rebuked, by the prophets, for its *dis*obedience to God, for its bad deeds. In the course of time there is a distinct change of emphasis: Israel makes a point of keeping the Law, of being noted for obedience and good deeds. It should be emphasized that adherence to the Law could be, and often was, the expression of great devotion.[6] But there is a latent danger. It is possible for the keeping of the Law to become the expression not of right-relatedness, but of self-reliance and self-justification. This is liable to be even more radically destructive of the relationship with God than is outright disobedience, especially since it *seems* to resemble the true relationship. This would be the proverbial self-righteousness of the Pharisee: righteousness that may be not merely independent of, but quite contrary to, right-relatedness with God. Good deeds do not automatically express right-relatedness.

It is being in relationship with God that is supremely important. However, this does not mean that such a relationship is free of ethical implications. One must, first, assert that self-justification—by 'works'—is irrelevant. To be redeemed is to enter into relation with God. But this relationship will express itself in goodness of behaviour, and if it did not do so, one might well question the reality of the relationship in the first place. Freedom from the 'Law' as a means of self-justification is *not* equivalent to lawlessness or licentiousness, as St Paul had to insist.[7] Doing cannot earn a state of being that it does not already express, but a state of being *will* in turn express itself by what it does. Historically, there has been a constant temptation to confuse the proper relation of the different levels of being and doing.

Entering the Christian life is not a matter of self-justification but of the forgiveness of sins. The person who is penitent is also the person who is forgiven. Man's penitence and God's forgiveness are the expression of the two sides of the new relationship. Penitence as an isolated quality would not be redemptive but only within the context of the relationship that is itself redemption.

At the same time, it is also important to note that without penitence the outworking of redemption would be checked, simply in that a person will not be saved against his will. It is God who saves, but it is man who in some sense must 'consent' to be saved, if salvation is to be actually achieved. Possibly this element of man's 'co-operation' has been insufficiently stressed by those who would—very rightly—insist on the priority of God's action or grace. One does not earn grace, and forgiveness is freely given, but at the same time there is a place for our response, for our willingness to accept what is offered. God wishes us to enter into relationship with him, and a real relationship requires the consent of both parties involved. Conversion is a personal act and cannot happen against our will, since this would in effect be a contradiction in terms. It is the idea of co-operation or *synergeia* which does justice to the reality of there being two sides in a genuine relationship. It does not imply even a partial attempt at self-justification, but points to the need for our response to what

God does, both at the entry to and throughout the Christian life. One does not *earn* God's love, but one does *respond* to it; and our capacity for responsiveness is one to be maintained and developed.

It is the relationship with God that is of fundamental importance, and all that one does should stem from this. The relation between being and doing should thus be raised in connection with the question of ministry. Here again there is the risk of assigning priority to doing, the temptation to let activity be a substitute for personal growth, instead of an authentic expression of such growth. But unless activity stems from the relationship with God, it may not truly be termed *Christian* ministry. One is to offer God not one's deeds, but oneself. Even altruism can be ambivalent. To 'do something for God' can be a matter of self-assertion, if isolated from the knowledge of what God has done for us and the relationship in which this is personally appropriated. The theology of ministry should not *begin* at the level of activity, since this is an inversion of priorities. The use of the term 'vocation' or 'call' must be applied first and foremost to entering into relationship with God: it is a matter of Christian *being* before it is a matter of Christian *doing*.

It may prove relevant to apply this particular distinction to the two sacraments of entry to the Christian life: baptism, and confirmation or chrismation. Whether or not the second sacrament immediately follows the first, there has often been confusion as to the relationship between the two. Does the second simply reaffirm the first, or is it really something additional in significance? I would like to suggest that, whatever else may be said of these sacraments, it may be helpful to see the first in terms of being and the second in terms of doing. Baptism marks the entry into relationship with Christ. This is basic. But confirmation or chrismation does not just reiterate this, though it does presuppose it. Given this basis, and only on this basis, the second sacrament goes on to commission and equip the Christian for service. In Orthodox terms this is 'lay ordination'. More generally speaking, it is the recognition that every Christian is called to some form of ministry, bearing in mind that there are many forms of ministry, just as there are many gifts of the Spirit.[8] Christian ministry is not a specialization for the few, but integral to the outworking of the relationship with Christ. The heresy of Christian activism, of doing not properly grounded in being, is well matched by the heresy of Christian inactivity—the idea that for many Christians being cannot be expected to express itself in any form of doing.

It should by now be apparent that the underlying point at issue is a singularly important one. The inability to understand the distinction and the inter-relation between being good and doing good has been a fruitful source of theological difficulties, with widespread ramifications into many areas of Christian thought. In particular, this question affects one's understanding of the relationship with God. But it affects much else besides.[9]

Growth in the Christian life is a continuing and ever-deepening movement of conversion. Penitence is the keynote. Growth to maturity, in relationship with God and with others in God, is the aim. Entry into a relationship with God is presupposed, and this remains a constant presupposition. What we are considering is not an attempt to earn such a relationship, but the development of the given relationship.

Penitence, as the option of guilty suffering which is involved in the restoration to goodness, comprises within itself a strong element of *realization*. One becomes aware, or more fully aware, of what one has done as being wrongful, and of the fact that it was oneself that did it. This is the pain of conscience. Awareness is complemented by acknowledgement and confession,[10] and the desire to turn from wrong is taken up by being forgiven and cleansed from it. However, there are different levels of cleansing in this process of growth. And, although growth implies the deepening of this cleansing, it does not imply that one stage must be fully worked through before the next is embarked upon. One stage is taken up by another. It is often assumed that the various stages are consecutive, but this is only true in the sense of one beginning before another. The most useful model would be one of interpenetrating levels. Thus, each level once it is begun may continue in greater or lesser degree for the rest of one's life. The need is for all that we have been and are to be cleansed, not just what we do and have done. The level of doing is only the level of effect and it is necessary to tackle the level of cause, which is that of being. In practice, it is the level of act and action which is tackled first, as being the more obvious and easily accessible. But the cleansing of our doing, though it may *begin* before the cleansing of our being, cannot be *completed* before this second and more radical cleansing, since what we do stems from what we are. The level of doing can by itself be only checked, not thoroughly cleansed. It is our whole being that is to be converted, not just one expression of it.

The model of two 'Dark Nights', one of the senses and one of the spirit, is descriptive of this deepening process of cleansing:

> In this purgation (sc. of the spirit) these two parts of the soul, the spiritual and the sensual, must be completely purged, *since the one is never truly purged without the other, the purgation of sense becoming effective when that of the spirit has fairly begun.* Wherefore the night which we have called that of sense may and should be called a kind of correction and restraint of the desire rather than purgation. The reason is that all the imperfections and disorders of the sensual part have their strength and root in the spirit, where all habits, both good and bad, are brought into subjection, and thus, until these are purged, the rebellions and depravities of sense cannot be purged thoroughly.[11]

The cleansing of the level of doing—or rather, the first stage of this cleansing, which will be carried further in the cleansing of the level of being—is the stage of *praxis* (= doing, activity). This is the 'active life', properly so-called, of religious terminology, precisely in that it involves dealing with the level of doing or activity. In effect it provides the spadework for further growth, by attempting to uproot faults and to develop virtues. Conversion does not imply 'fleeing the world' in the sense of abandoning or being exempted from the stresses of human existence. Redemption from sin is not to be equated with exemption from temptation. The struggle that is 'spiritual warfare'[12] is an intimate part of the process of conversion. To be tempted or tested provides opportunities for growth, so that all that one is may be offered to God and purified, and the whole person be converted. It is the testing that makes apparent what aspects of one's life still require to be brought into conversion. One has already entered into a relationship with God, and in that sense one is not unconverted. But maturity is not the instant accompaniment of new birth. It comes with the development of the relationship and, within this, with the increasing cleansing of what we do and are. Faults are to be checked and good actions are to be delivered from ambivalence—that is to say, the possibility that they, no less than specific faults, may be the expression of self-will. This *ascesis* or training is not to be seen as something negative, though. It is the *love* of God that cleanses one, and *ascesis* is not an end in itself, but only a means towards the goal of learning to love.

At all stages this cleansing takes place within the context of a relationship with God, not autonomously. However, just because this happens within a relationship, we may speak of the part played by each of the two sides of the relationship. Cleansing is often spoken of in terms of activity and passivity, of man's action and of God's action vis-à-vis man. It is these terms which need elucidation. In any case, neither aspect is to be detached from the other. There is the temptation to speak of activity, or man's action, as something autonomous. It is matched by the temptation to make passivity, or God's action vis-à-vis man, something independent of man's responsiveness. Each idea suggests that a relationship functions by the efforts of one side alone, irrespective of the response of the other—which is to deny the reality of relationship. In practice, activity and passivity interlink and are to be correlated with each other. The fact that God acts does not preclude but rather calls for man to respond and act in relationship. Passivity is not to be confused with inertia, but implies receptivity. At most it may be said that God's action may occasionally feel like passivity on our side, 'on the receiving end', as it were. But the important thing is not passivity as a state, but the fact of God's action vis-à-vis us, which may perhaps be experienced in terms of passivity, when it is specifically noticed at all. Our part is better described as responsiveness rather than passivity, since we are to be passive only vis-à-vis God, and not in abstraction. The term 'responsiveness' conveys this all-important connotation, and so should be helpful when the term 'passivity' may be misleading. Responsiveness is in fact descriptive of every level, as may be demonstrated by contrasting it with its contrary states. If one is self-active rather than responsive in doing, one has succumbed to activism. If one is merely passive and not actually responsive in being, one has succumbed to quietism. Both of these are autonomous states and hence self-centred. Each is to be remedied by the learning of responsiveness, which of itself implies other-centredness.

In that passivity implies responsiveness, it frequently leads to action in turn—action that is an expression of responsiveness. In effect this means that we use the word 'active' in two distinct ways. There is an important difference between the two uses, but unfortunately the fact of identical terminology has often led to neglect of this distinction, and indeed to the confusion of the two. On the one hand, there is *praxis*, activity in the sense of the cleansing of the level of doing. This is a preparation for, and leads on into, the cleansing of the level of being. On the other hand, there is activity in the sense of actions stemming from and expressing the level of being, which is being cleansed. *But it is former, and not the latter, which is properly the 'active life' of religious terminology*. The 'active life' is traditionally the struggle of spiritual warfare, or the first stage in the process of cleansing. It has nothing to do with the performance of actions, or activity in the more commonly understood sense. However, in the course of time, the proper meaning of the active life was confused with this second, more popular, understanding of activity. At the same time the contemplative life tended to be thought of as passivity incompatible with action, rather than as responsiveness that might involve action. This shift of meaning led to both the active and the contemplative lives being unduly defined by externals, and hence also to their being defined in opposition to each other. Properly speaking, the two are complementary: the active life leads into and is taken up by the contemplative life, in that both are stages in the development of one's relationship with God. Neither is in itself an occupational category; though either may sometimes *coincide* with such a category.

The second possible meaning of the word 'active' is part of what may be implied by the word 'contemplative', as understood in terms of responsiveness. If actions are not ambivalent but stem from the renewal of the level of being, they are themselves an expression of responsiveness. They are not opposed to contemplation, but may be an integral part of it. Indeed, using this second sense of the word 'active', it might well be true to say of a person that he or she is contemplative and *therefore* active. Ultimately, this may be realized in terms of St Teresa of Avila's well-known comment on the 'spiritual marriage'; 'This is the end of prayer, my daughters, this is what the spiritual marriage is for; from it are always born works, works!'[13] But responsiveness is also an essential characteristic of every step along the way, at every stage of growth in relationship.

In Orthodox terminology this capacity for responsiveness may be designated by the term *nepsis*, which is variously translated as vigilance, wakefulness, spiritual sobriety, or inward alertness. For responsiveness must be learned in terms of attentiveness; it is not to be assumed that the action of God will on any given occasion be specifically noticed. Responsiveness is not to be interpreted as a capacity to *feel* what is happening. This would be to reduce one's relationship with God to dependence on the state of one's emotions, while it is the response of the whole personality which is to be sought for and learned.

Attentiveness in turn requires one to learn the meaning of silence. The first and most obvious level of silence, the cessation of speech, must be supplemented by a more radical form of silence, beginning with the renunciation of concepts as well as of words. Any concept that one may have of God is less than God himself. Thus, the path to the knowledge of God must be one of 'knowing by unknowing', since all images and ideas keep one tied to the level of knowing *about* God, rather than that of knowing God. It is all concepts, and not just obviously false ones, that are less than the truth of the person, and hence these become a form of idolatry (= satisfaction with mere *images* of God) if they are accepted as a substitute for a first-hand relationship with God, who is greater than any image or concept of himself. The steadily increasing learning of silence—in which the 'attentiveness' of *nepsis* may ultimately become the 'stillness' of *hesychia*—is essential if one is not to succumb to this most subtle form of idolatry.

At the same time, the call to a first-hand relationship with God will to some extent be learned in terms of human aloneness. Silence and directness of contact cannot be learned if one avoids being alone with God, and human support may sometimes mask a fear of the inadequacy of the divine support, a fear to commit oneself unreservedly to the relationship. Hence in practice the reality of the divine support, and the capacity to trust in it, may to some extent have to be learned through the experience of the absence of human support and by the ability to 'stand alone', as it were. This is above all the pattern of the life of the solitary. But what the solitary particularly exemplifies is something that every Christian must learn, since for every Christian the aim is nothing less than this directness of contact. Having stated this, it should be added that for solitary and non-solitary alike this also proves to be the path to a deeper discovery of the experience of interdependence, not in fact the negation of it. Above all, both the aloneness and the radical silence are only significant as marks of growth in a relationship that is satisfied with nothing that is less than God himself.

We are not to allow any concept of God to become an idol, that is, a substitute for God. But the Christian life is an encounter with God both unknown and known, and we must also comment on the aspect of what is known and how this relates to what is unknown. Concepts may become idols, or they may be treated simply as pointers to the infinite reality of God. To deny the need for concepts altogether, in the hope of surpassing them, may lead one to lapse into sheer muddled thinking. This is not apophatic theology, reaching beyond conceptualization, but merely bad kataphatic theology, well within the level of the conceptual but doing less than justice to it. At a certain level there *is* conceptual knowledge of God, and the possibility of assertion, discussion, and the elimination of demonstrable error. This is possible, not as a matter of unwarranted pretensions of human reason, but because *God has chosen to reveal himself in history*—that is to say, within the ordinary conditions of human existence, thereby allowing himself to be in a real sense subject to the human modes of discussion and conceptualization. This is true of God's action in history generally; and supremely true of the incarnation, in which God committed a greater anthropomorphism than any man could commit, in that God in Christ *himself became man*. God by his own choice has been made known to us. But this of itself does not compel a relationship, and if we want first-hand contact with God who has thus acted, our conceptual knowledge *about* God must not be allowed to replace the reality of meeting and knowing God himself. Thus, in the Orthodox tradition the word *theologia* (= theology) refers primarily to the experience of union with God, not to conceptual knowledge, which is always less than, and may even be detached from, this actual relationship.[14] The integrated approach is expressed by Evagrius: 'If you are a theologian you will pray truly; and if you pray truly you are a theologian.'[15]

Reality in relationship is seen to necessitate the refusal to absolutize concepts. For man the exercise of renouncing images does in fact apply to both sides of the relationship. Not only must one let go of images of God; one must learn to abandon one's self-image, in the process of increasing self-knowledge and realization of oneself for what one truly is. One is to grow in the knowledge both of God and of oneself. It is this very process that is purgatorial. In essence it is the growth in love and cleansing of love that is and will be purgatory.

The symbols both of light and of darkness may be used as descriptive of the 'fire' of the love of God and its effect on those who have entered into relationship with God. The 'fire' is never to be quenched but will, with our transformation effected, be enjoyed by us for ever. The goal is union with God, a 'divinization' by grace that will at the same time be the full and true fulfilment of our humanity, as was the intention of man's creation in the image and likeness of God. The person thus transfigured will not however be a perfectionist, unable to relate to the condition of others. No, what we shall see is someone human and loving, capable of laughter and independence. In some such terms as these we shall be able to understand and apply the comment of St Irenaeus: 'The glory of God is a living man.'[16]

# 9
# Coinherence: All Life is Vicarious

Innocent suffering, just as guilty suffering, may be a matter of first-order suffering, i.e. it may be seen in terms of moral being. The innocent party bears the burden of his infliction. But the fact of burdens having been inflicted *by* others can be transformed: burdens may be borne *for* others. The sheer fact of infliction remains a fact; but in addition innocence may be taken up and transformed into vicariousness. The wrongdoer repudiates lateral responsibility and acts contrary to interdependence. However, the person wronged is not obliged to remain at the point of breakdown but may, through vicariousness, act laterally, towards the restoration of interdependence.

The basic form of innocence translated into vicariousness is that of forgiveness. Forgiveness is a change of heart in the wronged, vis-à-vis the wrongdoer. (A change of heart on the human level—with God it is the unchanging steadfastness of love.) The effect of forgiveness is thus to be seen firstly in the wronged—and sometimes only in the wronged, since forgiveness cannot compel the wrongdoer to change. Forgiveness may hope to beget a moral response in the wrongdoer, but it is not dependent on penitence, either as a prior condition or as a result; though on the other hand penitence may either precede forgiveness or be elicited by it. Forgiveness may happen to include the remission of an external penalty. However, whether or not it involves this, it is not to be seen in terms of cancellation without moral change. It does not imply a verdict of 'not guilty'. This would be condonation, or the acceptance of wrongdoing. Forgiveness implies acceptance of the wrongdoer as a person, but with full awareness of the horror of wrong (if there were not this awareness, what would there be to forgive?). Condonation would be to ignore the seriousness of wrongdoing and its consequences; it would be a lack of love, in that it would not imply any real concern for the other person's state. Condonation could never be redemptive. Forgiveness, as a mode of love and concern, may well be—though there is no compulsion in forgiveness, only the drawing power and attraction of love.

On the human level, we have to speak of both forgiveness and forgive*n*ness. We need to be forgiven, as well as to forgive. Forgiveness properly stems from forgive*n*ness. In particular, this is true of man's relationship with God. Entering this relationship may be seen in terms of forgive*n*ness, by the acceptance of God's forgiveness of us. This forgive*n*ness, or redemption, or restoration of love, is thus a new status of being, which is to express itself in forgiving. In other words, being loved should lead to loving in turn.

In the absence of forgiveness it is likely that the disruption of interdependence will be prolonged and the moral consequences of wrongdoing remain to some degree untransformed. And if the lack of forgiveness is allowed to breed resentment, this may in turn lead to retaliation. Thus, wrong suffered can lead to wrong done, and the innocent may in turn become the guilty, through responding in this way. Conversely, the guilty whom we have considered may once have been the innocent who responded to the infliction of wrong with resentment. In this way we have come full circle, back to our starting-point of wrongdoing committed. While not confusing innocence and guilt, it becomes evident that the relation between the two may be more complex that at first envisaged. Any given act of wrong may cause disruption of interdependence, but it may not be taken as necessarily the first point of such breakdown. We must in addition be aware of the possibility of earlier breakdown.

The guilty disrupt interdependence, but it would seem that interdependence was to some extent already disrupted. Precisely because we need to live from others as well as for them, one may not assume that a disruption in living *for* others is the only possible starting-point. Relating to people stems from the givenness of being related to, and if this derivation is disrupted it will of course have consequences for the personality and hence behaviour of the person thus affected. Those who act out alienation are often those who have been made alienated.

This is not to deny the responsibility of the wrongdoer for the wrong he commits. He *is* responsible, but he is not *solely* responsible. This is not a denial of individual responsibility. The linear principle, that we are responsible for what we have done, still holds good. But it is to assert that this cannot properly be taken as the only kind of responsibility in question, but should be seen against the larger background of the prior responsibility of other people. To deny that the individual alone is responsible is not to assert that others alone are responsible. We are contrasting the responsibility of the wrongdoer by himself with that of the wrongdoer together with other people. This is an inclusive, not exclusive, definition of corporate responsibility, so that the given individual is never left out altogether. Others may be responsible for creating a faulty relationship in the first place. This may be crystallized in one person, but he represents only one side of a faulty relatedness—the focal point of a bad situation, not its entirety. Thus, since a wrong action is often the outcome of a wrong situation, it may be illogical to blame one person only, the overt wrongdoer, without also allocating some blame to those who originated the faulty situation or rendered it intolerable. (It is not their responsibility only, but it is their responsibility also.) This must be qualified, of course, by stating that there is no determinism about this: people may overcome previous difficulties or refuse to act them out in a particular way. Conversely, the previous network of relationships may have been good, and yet a person thus sustained may choose to do wrong. Living from others does not of itself guarantee living for others, though without the former there are likely to be considerable difficulties in learning to live for others.

Fortunately, breakdown in one's original derivation need not be final. The unloved may subsequently be reached by the love of others, who were not the original unloving persons. The wrongdoer acts out a faulty relatedness on everyone, not just on the originators of this faulty relatedness. But, at the same time, the others who come to be involved—especially through being the wrongdoer's target—*may take up a responsibility they did not originate*. Prior responsibility for faulty relatedness is limited to certain given persons, who could have *not* done what has been done. Subsequent responsibility, however, is far broader and may be undertaken by anybody: it is the responsibility for *undoing* what has been done.

It is not enough to stop a person *doing* wrong, for what a person does is symptomatic of what he is. More positively, the goal is that of the restoration of relatedness, to be understood as both living from and living for others. Breakdown in derivation requires to be met by the attempt to restore the full functioning of interdependence. Mere segregation is no solution to isolation, if indeed it is isolation which the wrongdoer has acted out in terms of anti-social behaviour. The alternatives are the restoration of and reintegration into interdependence; or the taking of action which confirms or further aggravates the situation of broken interdependence. Outlawry and ostracism are typical of the approach which sees the wrongdoer as outside of interdependence and not to be reintegrated into it. Moreover, this is to disclaim any general responsibility for the malfunctioning of interdependence, and for having allowed a given person to become the focal point of this. The wrongdoer and the wrong committed are not seen as the outcome of a wrong situation. The current disruption of interdependence is stressed, and not any previous disruption which contributed to the present situation. This implies a confusion of cause and effect. The breakdown of interdependence, which has been led to manifest itself in wrongdoing, cannot be cured by prolonging the situation of breakdown, and punishment ought not to involve any continuation of what has already led the wrongdoer to act as he has done. It is the restoration of interdependence that must be the goal, and this will in turn manifest itself in acts of right-relatedness.

The person who has done wrong is to be punished. But when overt wrongdoing may be the outcome of a wrong situation, it makes sense to consider what steps might be taken to deal with it before it reaches the point of erupting in wrongdoing. This is the area, not of punishment, but of crime prevention. Crime prevention may be interpreted narrowly as a matter of taking measures to prevent potential criminals from acting. Or it may be understood more broadly and radically, as making the conditions of society such that people do not tend to develop into potential criminals. In particular, society may do much towards ensuring that its members do not suffer from breakdown in derivation, or being related to. For breakdown in living from others is always tragic, even when it does not lead on to crime. On the other hand, one has to bear in mind that even the provision of excellent conditions of derivation does not guarantee the proper functioning of interdependence, until the persons concerned also learn to live for others. In other words, they must recognize that other people need to live from them, and that the refusal to live for others necessitates a disruption in *their* derivation. The maintenance of complete derivation cannot take place unless all people learn to live for others. The two characteristics of interdependence cannot ultimately be separated from each other. One person lives from another because that other lives for him; and living for another in turn implies that that other is living from one. Interdependence is intended to function in terms of reciprocity. But reciprocity should be a matter of mutual consent; and short of this one should learn to forgive. Otherwise, if one bears resentment at lack of reciprocity, this aggravates the state of breakdown.

Early breakdown in interdependence may in fact lead to two rather different reactions. The person concerned may act out a resentment. Without forgiveness there may even be the insistence on 'one's rights' at all costs, i.e. the assertion of one set of rights to the exclusion of all others. Alternatively, there may be the compulsive attempt to *earn* the love that was not earlier given but that is so much needed. The attempt to earn love may or may not succeed, but in any case it would be preferable if it were forestalled, that is, forestalled by the *giving* of love. The earning of love is, in theological terms, comparable to the attempt at self-justification. One's attempt to live for others is not fully free or authentic if it has to be subordinated to the aim of earning what is not voluntarily given. Living for others can in this way be ambivalent. Seemingly, it is a more healthy and less troublesome response to broken interdependence than is the acting out of resentment. But when seen for what it truly is, is it really a better response? This may be compared to what we noted earlier: that outright disobedience, and obedience stemming from unrelatedness, are both contrary to true interdependence.[1] Both are unhealthy and, if anything, the latter is even more dangerous than the former, in that it so closely resembles the form of true interdependence while in essence being contrary to it. It is the restoration of interdependence that we are seeking, not the aping of it. (But whose is the fault if love is not given? . . .)

The principle of vicariousness is a means for the restoration of interdependence; and it is this precisely because it is first and foremost the normal expression of interdependence. All life is vicarious, in that it involves living from and for others. Vicariousness is not something esoteric, but the fundamental principle of all personal life. Self-centring is the destruction of life, in that personal life is not self-sufficient. The self-giving involved in vicariousness is not something necessitated by the condition of a sinful world, but is characteristic both of the path towards restoration and above all of the restoration itself. It is the *absence* of self-giving which marks the state of breakdown and its prolongation.

Vicarious suffering is but one category of the larger and more general principle of vicariousness.[2] Vicarious suffering does not stand alone, but presupposes the give and take of ordinary relatedness. The bearing of each other's burdens that is part of vicarious suffering must begin at the level of everyday helpfulness and concern; of courtesy and gratitude; of love for each other and prayer for each other. We shall regard vicariousness as merely esoteric or even incomprehensible if we neglect to see that it is, in its many forms, the basic principle of all personal life. It is precisely this neglect which has made it difficult for people to make sense of doctrines of the atonement, in that these have been relegated to the realm of the esoteric. Yet vicariousness is not abnormal, but the pre-eminently normal.

The learning of vicarious living, which is essential to the restoration of interdependence, is perhaps most specially characterized by the three 'evangelical counsels' of poverty, chastity, and obedience. These are not just a monastic prerogative. Because they involve interdependent qualities, they are able to provide guidelines for all life that is according to the image and likeness of God. Each will involve some form of detachment, as part of the unlearning of selfishness that is contrary to interdependence. But detachment is to be correlated with self-giving, in the process of learning to love.

The counsel of poverty will involve detachment from possessiveness vis-à-vis material objects. From possessiveness, not necessarily from possession as such, though the former is often to be learned in terms of the latter. Lack of possession is no guarantee of detachment, and possession does not necessitate possessiveness. In everyday terms non-possessiveness will imply generosity and sharing, the giving of gifts, and the stewardship of resources. The concept of 'gift' is particularly important. It is a potent reminder that we are to live from and for others, and that both immediately and ultimately what we 'have' is not a matter of possession. What we 'have' we have received from others, and we in turn are to give, so that others may receive from us. In neither respect should anything be considered our 'own'. The counsel of poverty is the recognition of this. It leads to sharing, both individually and collectively, as we realize our responsibility for others and understand that our life is from and for their life. To receive from others and acknowledge one's dependence on them—the fact that one is not self-sufficient—is to be understood in terms of the expression of love. The tragedy of self-sufficiency is the inability to receive love; and yet to be loved is more important than to possess for oneself, in unlovely isolation. Likewise, what one gives to others is more than the object that constitutes what is given. Essentially what one gives is love, or the gift of oneself. This is the fundamental gift, and all other gifts should be the expression of this.

At the same time, this non-possessiveness implies a respect for the whole material creation. To know the world as a gift is to preclude exploitation. Ecology and the concern for the environment stem naturally from this most fundamental recognition. Man was intended to be the steward of the material creation.[3] And ultimately 'the universe itself is to be freed from the shackles of mortality and enter upon the liberty and splendour of the children of God.'[4] We do not know in what terms this is to be realized; but we may at present remind ourselves that non-possessiveness thus assumes cosmic dimensions.

The material creation is what is tangibly available for giving to and receiving from each other. First and foremost, however, it is God's gift to us.[5] All that we may give or receive is ultimately from him. The world is the gift and sign of his love. At the same time, as a further sign of his love, he has included in his gift the possibility of further giving and receiving, and the capacity for thanksgiving and the reciprocation of love. It is from the counsel of poverty that our recognition of this stems.

The counsel of chastity will involve detachment from possessiveness vis-à-vis people. It does not imply non-relatedness. However, relatedness is all too often marred by possessiveness and even exploitation, which are part of the breakdown of interdependence. One may either lack concern for others, or one's concern may be marred by self-will and the attempt to relate to other people on one's own terms. It is the healing and renewal of personal relationships that is integral to this counsel. The love that is being freed from narrowness and self-centredness will include a special concern for the unloved and for those who are not yet able to reciprocate love. The detachment involved in non-possessiveness proves to be a basis for truer and wider self-giving.

The attitude to specifically sexual relationships is to be set within this wider context. Chastity is not in any case to be equated with celibacy. Chastity is a broader term, referring both to celibacy as such and to sexual relationships that are truly committed and loving, of which marital fidelity is intended to be the norm or paradigm. This is to say that chastity is concerned with the fulfilment of sexual relationships, as well as with abstinence from such relationships. Celibacy is a valid and valuable option, but it is not the only option, and chastity is certainly not to be equated with a disregard for sexual love or condemnation of it. This would be to adopt the approach of dualism, which is radically contrary to the Christian understanding of the material creation. Because Christianity is the religion of the incarnation, of the Word made flesh, it has a positive estimate of materiality, and hence the kind of fundamental basis for a positive approach to sexuality that cannot be paralleled by any non-incarnational understanding.

Finally, there is the counsel of obedience, calling for the response of man's will to the will of God. Our whole personality is to be redirected from egoism to God-centredness and, in God, to true responsiveness to all other beings. Obedience, as responsiveness to others, is above all an interdependent quality. To obey someone is to live for him.

> The essence of obedience is to be able to understand, to catch the thought and will of the neighbour, and by the movement of love to realize this power and this will ... If someone is ill spiritually, in that fallen state, he is unable to follow the will of his neighbour, and so he lives self-centredly.[6]

But the fact that our obedience is primarily to God implies that we may not obey the fallen will of our neighbour, but should respond only to whatever his real need may be. Genuine acceptance of a person does not imply a lack of concern for his true welfare. Love seeks to elicit a response of love from the person it loves. It does not seek to impose good behaviour on its beloved, for this is something lesser. And, if good behaviour does not stem from the right-relatedness of love, it is in any case ambivalent and inauthentic.

Obedience implies attentiveness, without which one cannot hope to perceive the needs of one's neighbour. It is not necessarily a matter of being specifically asked to do something. One must learn to be perceptive to needs both asked and unasked. Obedience involves the learning of accuracy in love. It is possible to be both able and willing to do something, but this is insufficient without knowledge and understanding of the situation. Obedience is therefore the opposite of insensitivity, which seeks to act on its own terms and according to its own ideas about a situation. Accuracy in love implies our willingness to let go of our own preconceived ideas and our understanding of 'what is best'. Often it does not imply more than this. We may or may not come to understand a situation, but God does understand it fully, and our part is to acknowledge this and to entrust a person or situation into his hands, without imposing our own diagnosis or solution. Accuracy in love does not imply our own omniscience, still less the satisfaction of every curiosity. It is the abandoning of self-will in the realm of understanding.

Obedience proves to be a more radical and demanding quality than is usually recognized. It should involve one's whole self and not just one's actions, i.e. all that one is, as well as all that one does. This is given firstly to God, and under God to all other people. It is not basically a matter of obeying one person alone, except insofar as this may serve as a means to the wider end. Obedience to a spiritual parent is a training for obedience in its more radical sense.

The spiritual father or spiritual mother is *par excellence* an obedient person. They may help others to be obedient because they have learned obedience themselves. They speak and act not from a position of their own authority, but from that of continuing obedience. The director of spiritual parent and spiritual child alike is the Holy Spirit. It is through the experience of obedience, and the discernment that stems from obedience, that the spiritual parent may help his spiritual child—by word, by example, and above all by intercession: The abba was the one who, really knowing God in his own experience, could most truly intercede for his sons.'[7] Intercession may be specifically linked with obedience: 'Without obedience we cannot pray for other people—if I am disobedient I cannot catch the suffering and tragedy of my neighbour or understand his need: therefore without obedience I cannot pray for him.'[8] The purpose of the relationship between spiritual parent and spiritual child is to enable the spiritual child to grow to maturity in Christ, which is true human maturity. The training is geared to a first-hand relationship with God, not to dependency on the spiritual parent and still less to satisfaction with religious experience received at second-hand. For the spiritual parent realizes that ultimately it is not his or her own spiritual child, but—like himself or herself—a child of God, adult and free.

The evangelical counsels are means of learning interdependence and vicarious living. Each may be understood in terms of kenosis, the self-emptying that is involved both in detachment and in self-giving. This self-emptying is to be the underlying principle of all Christian living. It may at times take on spectacular forms: folly for Christ[9] is one of the means of demonstrating the eschatological tension between the life of the 'fallen' world and the life of the Kingdom of God. Acceptance of conventions and common sense may give way to the senseless, the ridiculous, the shocking, and the mad. But when the underlying motivation is truly the love of Christ, this is but one way of pinpointing the perennial paradox:

> As God in his wisdom ordained, the world failed to find him by its wisdom, and he chose to save those who have faith by the folly of the Gospel.[10]

Self-emptying as an interdependent quality is primarily learned and exercised in the give and take of living with others: 'It is the common life that provides the primary means of self-loss'.[11] But communal life as such is not the only means of undertaking interdependent living. There is also the life of the solitary. Although involving withdrawal from one level of relating to people, it does not imply withdrawal from coinherence as such, but reaffirms it at a deeper level. This should be true of all forms of interdependence, but is by no means always so. Even when the dimension of interdependence in God is present, it may sometimes be masked or not fully realized. The solitary life is thus a reassertion of priorities: it seeks the realization of man's interdependence in God, and it does so uncompromisingly. By denying itself immediate human contact, it allows itself only that level of interdependence that is manifestly in God—for in purely human terms it has no means of human contact. In this way the ideal of interdependence in God which should be true of all relatedness is focused in, and particularly exemplified by, the solitary life. It is a witness to what should be true of all human life.

The solitary life is, paradoxically, a true form of interdependent living. It is to be contrasted with the forms of the breakdown of interdependence, and in particular with the consummation of this breakdown that would be hell. Geographical isolation, even though this may involve a measure of emotional loneliness, need not be in any way contrary to interdependence. Moral and spiritual isolation, even when in close proximity with others, is intrinsically contrary to interdependence.

The life of solitude will normally follow a period of preparation and training in obedience within the context of communal living. *Interdependent* living is the primary means of self-loss; and this is to be learned in the context of community living, if it is not to be merely fanciful in the stage of solitary living. The solitary life provides less of the obvious opportunities for the responsiveness of obedience that communal life provides. Hence the would-be solitary must have learned obedience. Solitude is not to be a matter of self-will, but of selfless responsiveness to the Holy Spirit. It is not the aloneness of someone enclosed in himself, but an aloneness that is rooted in God and authentically interdependent.

The solitary pinpoints every man's total dependence on God by deriving all the support of his life from God without any evident human support, which perhaps conceal this total dependence. He or she exemplifies every Christian's quest for a first-hand relationship with God and directness of contact, which may be learned in terms of ever-deepening levels of silence and—to a greater or lesser extent—of solitude. Solitary and non-solitary alike are to grow in penitence and compassion, in intercession and general vicariousness. The solitary life in particular presupposes a degree of stability and constancy in prayer, since it has nothing to fall back on which might perhaps mask a failure in prayer. But stability is not to be confused with ease and absence of struggle. It is the solitary above all who has to enter into the heart of the struggle, both in terms of his or her own growth and cleansing, and as a channel of reconciliation for the needs and shortcomings of the whole world:

> The solitary, from his standpoint of simple dependence, is ... to give himself to be a channel of the divine mercy for the world. As the natural creative energies of his life are transfigured by the recreative energies of the Spirit, the discord, rebellion, and falling short of the natural world are held by his prayer to the judgement and healing of Christ's redeeming love.[12]

The solitary life has a vital role to play in the restoration of interdependence.

All our interdependence is intended to be interdependence in God. Intercession is the general expression of this, and indeed it is paradigmatic of all forms of vicariousness. It is by definition an interdependent act, and its significance derives naturally from the overall principle of interdependent living. It is sometimes asked why there is any need for intercession. If God knows of a particular situation, and is concerned for it, and is able to act, why do we need to pray about it? But if this question is raised, another question suggests itself. Why should one ever do anything for anybody?—since it remains true that God knows of the need, is concerned about it, and able to act. Intercession is not to be divorced from other expressions of vicariousness, and the same question ought to be asked in each instance. But in the latter more general instance, the question would hardly be considered worth asking. We take it for granted that we have the capacity to give and to receive, to help and to be helped, in everyday life. Rightly so, since God created us to live from and for each other, and without this interdependence there would be no personal life. One cannot suggest that intercession is superfluous without implicitly attacking the fact of interdependence as such. To ask about the need for intercession is to touch on something much larger and more fundamental: the question of why God created us interdependent, after his own likeness.

The interdependent life is to be one of mutuality, exchange, and reciprocity; of giving and receiving; of living so completely from and for others that nothing is left of self-centredness. Interdependence restored can be no less than eternal life. This we may enter into here and now;[13] we may have a genuine foretaste and experience of whatever it may ultimately be. In what ways, though, may we think of heaven? There is, first, the idea of the 'communion of saints'. This is by definition expressive of interdependence: it is the communion of all who are related in Christ, here and now as well as there and then. Man's solidarity with man is most truly realized when it is a solidarity in God. Man is not saved alone; salvation has this corporate dimension, since we are not isolated individuals, but interdependent, in the likeness of the Trinity.

Heaven may also be said to involve the pronouncement of what we have become, for good. The desert of goodness is not external, but the intrinsic bliss of self-giving and self-emptying. Kenosis is not a means to 'gain admission' to heaven. It is heaven's very essence. Those who have not learned to love will be intrinsically incapable of enjoying heaven. Those who have learned to love will in fact *be* 'in heaven'. But heaven will also be continually more and greater. It is not something static, but as it were progressive.[14] Our hunger for God will be satisfied, not with satiety, but with an ever greater hunger and an ever greater satisfaction, and hunger again. And thus unceasingly.

God himself is the bliss of heaven, and thus our final thought will be that of the vision of God, the beatific vision. Love himself will be seen, and known, and loved, beyond all measure. We cannot describe or predict the terms in which this may be realized. We will, however, conclude with an image that may point to something of the loveliness of what is and ever shall be:

> I saw in my imagination heaven, and our Lord as the head of his own house, who had invited all his dear servants and friends to a great feast. The Lord, I saw, occupied no one place in particular in his house, but presided regally over it all, suffusing it with joy and cheer. Utterly at home, and with perfect courtesy, himself was the eternal happiness and comfort of his beloved friends, the marvellous music of his unending love showing in the beauty of his blessed face. Which glorious countenance of the Godhead fills heaven full of joy and delight.[15]

# Postscript: Some Conclusions

The question of suffering is a fundamental one, and in some form or other underlies much of the presentation of the doctrine of the atonement. In particular, it affects the interpretation of what Christ did. Christ, the innocent, suffered for us, the guilty. But to what extent has Christ's admittedly innocent suffering been interpreted within a framework of guilty suffering? Christ's suffering has sometimes been interpreted in terms of punishment ('Christ bore our punishment') or penitence ('Christ the perfect penitent'). But each of these is a matter of guilty suffering—punishment obviously so, and penitence likewise when understood as a referent of punishment and type of 'first-order' guilty suffering. However, if innocent suffering is interpreted in terms of guilty suffering, there is a risk of confusion, and one may for this reason find such theories inadequate or even repugnant. I do not wish to assert that these theories had or have no possible value, but would feel it necessary to point out this notable limitation in them.

In any case, there is in contemporary thought a widespread loss of understanding of the meaning of guilty suffering and of punishment in particular. This general problem in turn renders it difficult for theology to maintain any vital understanding of guilty suffering, and thus automatically devalues theological theories which presuppose some aspect of this. We have devoted much space to the quest for the rediscovery of the meaning of guilty suffering, and hope by so doing to have provided a means for the re-evaluation and criticism of existing theories. The distinction between punishment and its referents proves to be of particular importance.

Atonement is also linked with eschatology, in that this marks an aspect of the outworking of the atonement. If the atonement is truly decisive, it is ultimately decisive, and one may not accept interpretations of eschatology that are contrary to what is implied by the atonement—which in any case may itself be understood as inaugurated eschatology. Eschatology is more than just 'the afterlife', but we have included a reassessment of concepts of the afterlife, through the application of conclusions already drawn from the discussion of guilty suffering.

It has been necessary to elucidate the process of differentiation between guilty and innocent suffering, and to establish firmly the distinction between the two. Our 'problem of *innocent* suffering' is neither universal nor normative. It is a very considerable achievement to recognize the fact of genuinely innocent suffering, and sometimes this recognition is not attained. However, unless one acknowledges the possibility of innocent suffering, one has no conceivable basis for the recognition of vicarious suffering, which is central to the Christian understanding of redemption.

In addition, this is yet another factor that has created difficulties for atonement theories interpreted in terms of guilty suffering. The attempt has been made to speak of representation or mediation or some similar expression of vicariousness, but this has again been done within a framework of guilty suffering—not of innocent suffering, as would be proper for vicariousness. For instance, it may be misleading to speak of the substitution of the innocent for the guilty in punishment, since this would seem to be injustice. Likewise, one might feel some reserve about using the concepts of vicariousness and penitence in conjunction with each other. But one may speak of substitution—or, better, representation—within the broader context of interdependence, in such a way that the action of the innocent on behalf of the guilty is not compromised in its interpretation. A 'substitutionary' theory of the atonement is certainly possible, but care must be taken as to the way in which this is expressed. If substitution is understood in linear terms—that is, of guilty suffering—the risk is of inaccuracy and injustice. But it may properly be understood laterally, as a matter of innocence and vicariousness.

We have also approached vicariousness from the consideration of goodness and its desert. Goodness is not to be envisaged as something static, but implies self-emptying; and it is essentially its own reward. Thus, we have approached vicariousness by means of two propositions. One is that there is genuinely innocent suffering (not all suffering is guilty suffering). The other is that the righteous may not only be rewarded, but may also suffer. Indeed if the reward of righteousness is basically none other than the intrinsic reward of self-emptying, there need no longer be any logical difficulty in the proposition that the righteous may suffer.

Interdependence or coinherence or vicariousness is the constant presupposition of our discussion. This understanding of man is to be linked with the trinitarian monotheism that is the distinctively Christian understanding of God. Man was created as interdependent, 'in the image' of God.* Interdependence is the essential dynamic of personal existence. But it can be, and has been, abused, and there is need for restoration. Vicariousness itself proves to be both the goal and the means to the goal. It is not esoteric, but the fundamental characteristic of normal human life, as properly understood. Man is to be redeemed by and into vicarious living. Interdependence may be restored by the means of interdependence.

The term 'redemption' is itself capable of a variety of interpretations. Vicariousness, and vicarious suffering in particular, have been singled out as key concepts. They are characteristic of the Christian understanding, and to a large extent distinctive of it, at any rate in their developed form. The restoration of interdependence may be contrasted with the goals of self-salvation and self-perfection. Likewise, this may provide a fuller solution than is usual to some of the data of the problem of suffering. Interdependence restored is more than just the cessation of suffering *per se*, and it certainly does not imply the loss of the *capacity* for suffering.

The atonement is to be worked out in human lives. Hence we are to ask not only about what Christ did, but how this works out in and for us. Christ lived and died and rose again *for us*. It is argued that a balanced doctrine of the atonement should include consideration of its outworking and appropriation.

Redemption is the restoration of creation to the purposes of its creator. It is important to be aware of the kind of questions to which the atonement is the 'answer'. In our discussion we have felt free to use both natural theology, understood as the language

---

*This analogy of course is and always has been subject to certain qualifications. It is not intended to minimize the distinction between God and his creation; nor should it be pressed to the point of suggesting tritheism.

of the theology of creation, and the specific theology of redemption. It is hoped that this twofold perspective will have been of particular help for our stated purpose of elucidating the presuppositions of the doctrine of the atonement.

# Special Note

## R. C. MOBERLY ON PUNISHMENT AND ITS RELATION TO PENITENCE

Some material is provided here for those who may be interested to trace the connections between the thought of R. C. Moberly and that of Sir Walter Moberly.

From *Atonement and Personality*
See especially ch. 1: Punishment, and ch. 11: Penitence.

> pp. xvii–xviii. Punishment is meant to be transmuted into penitence; and it is only as penitence that it has any restorative or atoning quality.

> p. 10. ... sin means a condition of a personality, and ... punishment is a treatment of a personality.

> p. 15. ... it is well to remember that infliction from without, by another, so far from being an essential element in all thought of punishment, tends more and more completely to disappear ... in those deeper realities of punishment, which human punishings do but outwardly symbolize.

> p. 15. The more we discern their process and character, the more profoundly do we recognize that the punishments of God are what we should call self-acting. There is nothing in them that is arbitrary, imposed, or, in any strict propriety of the word, inflicted ... what is called the judgement of God upon sin is but the gradual necessary development, in the consistent sinner, of what sin inherently is.

> p. 15. The whole progress of sin is a progressive alienation from God; and the climax of such a progressive alienation is that essential incompatibleness with God which we call hell.

> p. 16. It is of considerable importance to insist upon this spontaneous or inherent character of the consequence of sin ...

p. 18. ... there is no element of outward infliction which may not minister to sorrow of conscience.

p. 23. Either the suffering of punishment is more and more absolutely identified with penitential painfulness; or it has nothing atoning or restorative about it.

p. 30. ... on the one hand the whole system of external punishment; on the other the whole history and process of inner anguish of soul.

p. 34. Now it is characteristic of real moral evil, as of real moral good, that it cannot but affect the character of the self ...

p. 36. ... penalty is capable of translation into penitence.

p. 131. What would have been punishment *till it became penitence*, is, in the perfectly contrite, only as penitence. It is true that penitence is a condition of suffering. The suffering of penitence may quite fairly be termed penal suffering ... To the penitent, in proportion as he is perfected, there is no punishment *outside* his penitence.

p. 278. ... in proportion to its true working, (punishment) is itself superseded and absorbed. It becomes an aspect or mode of something which is beyond, yet is characterized by, itself. The proper goal of penal pain is the consummation of penitence.

From *Sorrow, Sin and Beauty*
Bodily suffering as important for its influence on the personality.

p. 18. ... the true place of the agony of bodily suffering is, to man at least, in the conscious and reflecting mind.

p. 18. ... it is at all events certain that bodily pain is in numberless ways affected for good or for evil by that reflecting consciousness and knowledge of the sufferer, in which alone it has, for us, its reality.

p. 19. Something clearly is needed for the refining besides the mere fact of pain.

p. 21. The refinement is not really a refinement of the body through bodily conditions, but a refinement and an education, through mental conditions and processes, of the mind. Here it is that the real presence of the suffering, the working of the suffering, the flower and fruit of the suffering, are to be found.

p. 22. Sorrow revolted against is sorrow profitless. But with the gradual acceptance begins also its transforming power.

p. 154. We shall incur only that which we shall *be*; we ourselves shall have wrought out the terms of our own judgement . . .

# References and Notes

## CHAPTER 1

1. Genesis 1.27.
2. Romans 12.4, 5.
3. P. Teilhard de Chardin, *Human Energy*, p. 152.
4. *Letter* 8 of St Basil. The author of the letter was actually Evagrius Ponticus.
5. A common phrase in fourth-century writers.
6. St Luke 9.24 (AV).
7. Relation, rather than relationship, since no specific connection between the two is being presupposed beyond the fact of their both being involved in the act of wrongdoing.
8. Bk. v, ch. 3. Dostoevsky's own position may not be summarized solely from his description of Ivan Karamazov, but it is interesting to note that he himself spoke of Ivan's argument as 'irrefutable'. To Lyubimov, *Pisma* IV, p. 53.
9. In a talk to a group of Dominicans, reported in *La Vie Intellectuelle*, April 1949.
10. Ibid. Cf. *La Peste*, p. 240, where Dr Rieux disagrees with the priest, Father Paneloux.
11. John Hick, *Evil and the God of Love*.

## CHAPTER 2

1. Philippians 2.7.
2. St Irenaeus, *Adversus Haereses*, III.18.1.
3. Ephesians 1.10.
4. *Adv. Haer.*, III.18.7.
5. Ibid., V.16.2.
6. St Matthew 4.1 ff.; St Luke 4.1 ff.; Hebrews 2.18, 4.15, 5.8.
7. *Adv. Haer.*, III.18.6. See also also III.18.7, III.21.10, V.16.3, which quote from St Paul.
8. Ibid., IV.39.1.
9. See in particular *Adv. Haer.*, V.27.2.
10. Ibid., V.15.1, V.21.3.
11. 2 Peter 1.4.; 1 Corinthians 1.9; Galatians 2.20; Ephesians 3.19; 1 John 1.3.
12. *Adv. Haer.*, V.1.1.
13. Ephesians 1.10.
14. *Adv. Haer.*, III.21.9.
15. Ibid., V.32.1.
16. St John 1.14.

## REFERENCES AND NOTES

17. *Adv. Haer.*, v.14.2.
18. Ibid., v.10.1. My emphasis.
19. Ibid., v.1.1.
20. Romans 1.19, 20.
21. *Adv. Haer.*, v. preface. See also III.10.2, III.19.1, v.16.2, v.36.3.
22. St Clement of Alexandria, *Protrepticon* 1.8.4; St Athanasius, *De Incarnatione* 54; St Gregory of Nazianzus, *Oratio* 29.19; St Gregory of Nyssa, *Oratio Catechetica* 25, 37; St Maximus the Confessor, *Ambigua* 125.
23. Peter Abelard, *Commentary on Romans*, II.3.26, II.5.6, II.5.7–8; *Epitome* 23.
24. L. W. Grensted, *A Short History of the Doctrine of the Atonement*, p. 105.
25. G. Aulén, *Christus Victor*, p. 146.
26. *Epitome* 34.
27. Peter Abelard, *Ethics* 3.
28. Ibid.
29. Ibid.
30. Ibid.
31. *Ethics* 18.
32. *Ethics* 20.
33. *Ethics* 19. See also *Ethics* 16.
34. J. G. Sikes, *Peter Abailard*, p. 179.
35. *Commentary on Romans*, II.3.26, II.5.6, III.8.34; *Epitome* 23; *Letter* 5.
36. *Comm. Rom.*, II.5.9; *Letter* 5.
37. *Comm. Rom.*, II.5.7–8, II.5.9.
38. *Comm. Rom.*, II.3.26, II.5.6; *Epitome* 23.
39. *Epitome* 23.
40. *Ethics* 3.
41. *Epitome* 23.
42. Ibid.
43. E.g. *Comm. Rom.*, II.3.26, where both the incarnation and the passion are also mentioned.
44. *Epitome* 23, where again this is part of a discussion which speaks of, and indeed links, the incarnation and the passion.
45. *Comm. Rom.*, II.5.7–8.
46. *Comm. Rom.*, II.3.26.
47. *Epitome* 23.
48. *Epitome* 23, two references.
49. *Comm. Rom.*, II.3.26, II.5.6.
50. *Comm. Rom.*, II.5.7–8; *Epitome* 23.
51. L. W. Grensted, op. cit., p. 107.
52. *Comm. Rom.*, II.3.25; *Epitome* 23.
53. *Comm. Rom.*, II.5.7–8.
54. *Epitome* 23; *Comm. Rom.*, II.3.26.
55. 1 Corinthians 13.12.
56. *Adv. Haer.*, IV.20.7.
57. Ibid., IV.20.5–6. See also IV.38.3.
58. See above, p. 18.
59. *Adv. Haer.*, IV.12.2, commenting on 1 Corinthians 13.
60. G. Aulén, L. W. Grensted, H. Rashdall, J. G. Sikes, R. E. Weingart.
61. *Letter* v.

## CHAPTER 3

1. St John 5.24. The qualitative nature of eternal life was reaffirmed by F. D. Maurice in the well-known controversy of the nineteenth century. An account of this may be found in G. Rowell, *Hell and the Victorians*, pp. 76–89.
2. The first and fourth of the Four Noble Truths of Buddhism.
3. Christmas Humphreys, *Buddhism*, p. 115.
4. Ibid., p. 103.
5. His Holiness the Dalai Lama, at a discussion in Oxford in autumn 1973.
6. Ananda K. Coomaraswamy, *Buddha and the Gospel of Buddhism*, p. 233.
7. *Buddhism*, p. 103.
8. H. S. Olcott, *Fundamental Buddhistic Beliefs*, no. 12. Quoted in *Buddhism*, p. 73.
9. *Buddhism*, p. 102. My emphasis of the last clause.
10. Ibid., p. 160.
11. Job 31.3.
12. Job 31.16–20.

## CHAPTER 4

1. For the purposes of this discussion I do not consider it necessary to elaborate the distinction between sin—which is admittedly a broader and specifically theological term—and wrongdoing. I will speak primarily in terms of wrongdoing, because this is something more precise and concrete, and because I wish to go on to consider criminological theory. But, *mutatis mutandis*, I wish the discussion to be taken to apply to sin and wrong generally.
2. Ezekiel 18.2.
3. Ezekiel 18.20.
4. Romans 5.12.
5. St Matthew 5.38, 39.

## CHAPTER 5

1. Sir Walter Moberly, *The Ethics of Punishment*, p. 12.
2. Op. cit., ch. 6.
3. Spinoza, *Ethics*, pt. v, xlii.
4. *The Ethics of Punishment*, p. 159.
5. Ibid., p. 164.
6. Ibid., p. 164.
7. Ibid., p. 179.
8. Ibid., p. 182.
9. Ibid., p. 183.
10. Ibid., p. 184.
11. Ibid., p. 185.
12. Op. cit., ch. 7.
13. Ibid., p. 189.
14. Ibid., p. 12.

15. Ibid., p. 191.
16. Ibid., p. 196.
17. Ibid., p. 198.
18. Ibid., p. 199.
19. Ibid., p. 200.
20. Ibid., p. 202.
21. Ibid., p. 203.
22. Ibid., p. 203.
23. Ibid., p. 203.
24. Ibid., pp. 203-4.
25. Ibid., p. 205. My emphasis.
26. Ibid., p. 205.
27. Ibid., p. 208.
28. Ibid., p. 208.
29. Ibid., p. 212.
30. Ibid., p. 215.
31. Ibid., p. 217. My emphasis.
32. Ibid., pp. 218-19.
33. Ibid., p. 219.
34. Ibid., p. 219.
35. Ibid., p, 222.
36. Ibid., p. 202.
37. Ibid., p. 202.
38. Lord Denning, 'Report of the Royal Commission on Capital Punishment', s.53. Cf. A. C. Ewing (*The Morality of Punishment*) who speaks of punishment as an expression of moral condemnation.

# CHAPTER 6

1. I. Kant, *The Philosophy of Law*, pt. II, pp. 194-5.
2. F. H. Bradley, *Ethical Studies*, p. 26.
3. I. Kant, *Lectures on Ethics*, p. 55.
4. G. Hegel, *Philosophy of Right*, p. 247; 64: para. 101.
5. J. M. E. McTaggart, *Studies in Hegelian Cosmology*, p. 129.
6. Ibid., p. 130.
7. H. B. Acton, ed., *The Philosophy of Punishment*, p. 15.
8. Ted Honderich, *Punishment*, p. 26.
9. G. Hegel, op. cit., p. 71, para. 101.
10. Ibid., p. 247; 64: para. 101.
11. See above, p. 83.
12. B. Bosanquet, *Some Suggestions in Ethics*, p. 190.
13. G. Hegel, op. cit., p. 69, para. 99.
14. Ibid., p. 70, para. 99.
15. Ibid., p. 248; 66: para. 104.
16. B. Bosanquet, *The Philosophical Theory of the State*, p. 226.
17. J. M. E. McTaggart, op. cit., p. 135.
18. F. H. Bradley, op. cit., p. 26.
19. Ibid., p. 26.

20. Herbert L. Packer, 'The Practical Limits of Deterrence', in R. J. Gerber and P. D. McAnany, eds., *Contemporary Punishment*, p. 105.
21. Ted Honderich, op. cit., p. 148.
22. Beccaria, *Dei delitti e delle pene*, 1. Quoted in Coleman Phillipson, *Three Criminal Law Reformers*, p. 57.
23. Sir Walter Moberly, *The Ethics of Punishment*, pp. 43–4.
24. Jeremy Bentham, *An Introduction to the Principles of Morals and Legislation*, I.1, p. 11.
25. Ibid., III.1, p. 34.
26. J. S. Mill, *Examination of Sir William Hamilton's Philosophy*, p. 510.
27. Anthony M. Quinton, 'On Punishment', in H. B. Acton, ed., *The Philosophy of Punishment*, p. 61.
28. Jeremy Bentham, *The Theory of Legislation*, p. 338.
29. John Plamenatz, *The English Utilitarians*, p. 92.
30. Garafalo, *Criminology*, p. 256. Quoted in Francis A. Allen, 'Criminal Justice, Legal Values, and the Rehabilitative Ideal', in Stanley E. Grupp, ed., *Theories of Punishment*, p. 325.
31. Francis A. Allen, art. cit., p. 325.
32. R. J. Gerber and P. D. McAnany, eds., *Contemporary Punishment*, pp. 130–31.
33. Helen Silving, 'The Dual-track System: Punishment and Prevention', in *Contemporary Punishment*, p. 144.
34. Ibid., p. 144.
35. Stanley I. Benn and Richard S. Peters, 'The Utilitarian Case for Deterrence', in *Contemporary Punishment*, p. 97.
36. J. M. E. McTaggart, op. cit., p. 131. My emphasis.
37. Sheldon Glueck, 'Principles of a Rational Penal Code', in *Theories of Punishment*, p. 277.
38. Stanley I. Benn and Richard S. Peters, art. cit., pp. 97–8.
39. Jeremy Bentham, *Principles of Penal Law*, p. 396.
40. Stanley I. Benn and Richard S. Peters, art. cit., p. 98.
41. Marc Ancel, 'New Social Defense', in *Contemporary Punishment*, p. 138.
42. H. Rashdall, *The Theory of Good and Evil*, vol. 1, p. 306.
43. Helen Silving, art. cit., p. 141.
44. Marc Ancel, art. cit., p. 134.
45. B. Bosanquet, *The Philosophical Theory of the State*, p. 223.

# CHAPTER 7

1. Sir Walter Moberly, *The Ethics of Punishment*, p. 205. My emphasis.
2. This idea of the priority of the good will for the Christian be linked with the existence of God. Here it is sufficient for it to be considered as the common presupposition of criminological thought.
3. *The Ethics of Punishment*, p. 219.
4. Ibid., p. 221.
5. The 'leprosy analogy'. See above, p. 77.
6. See above, p. 34.

# REFERENCES AND NOTES

7. For the concept of 'realized' or 'inaugurated' eschatology, see C. H. Dodd, *Parables of the Kingdom* and W. G. Kummel, *Promise and Fulfilment*.
8. *The Ethics of Punishment*, ch. 13.
9. Ibid., p. 341.
10. Ibid., p. 351.
11. Ibid., p. 353.
12. St Catherine of Genoa, *Purgatory*, ch. III.
13. Ibid., ch. II.
14. Ibid., ch. X.
15. R. C. Moberly, in W. Sanday, ed., *Priesthood and Sacrifice*, p. 106.
16. R. C. Moberly, *Atonement and Personality*, p. 129.
17. Ibid., pp. 39, 117.
18. Ibid., p. 129.
19. Ibid., p. 39.
20. Ibid., pp. 42–3.
21. Ibid., p. 117. See also *Priesthood and Sacrifice*, p. 125.
22. In *Priesthood and Sacrifice*, p. 128.
23. *Atonement and Personality*, p. 43.
24. Ibid., p. 47.
25. Ibid., p. 151.
26. Ibid., p. 47.
27. Ibid., p. 248.

# CHAPTER 8

1. Latin *converto* = I turn.
2. A use preserved in the Orthodox Church, though often an historical memory elsewhere.
3. St Gregory of Sinai, *Chapters*, 113.
4. Mother Mary Clare, S.L.G., *Christian Maturity through Prayer*, p. 9.
5. An idea typical of Theophan the Recluse. In *The Art of Prayer*, tr. E. Kadloubovsky and G. E. H. Palmer, p. 63 and *passim*.
6. Consider for instance the beauty of Psalm 119.
7. Romans 6.1, 15; Galatians 5.13.
8. 1 Corinthians 12.4 ff.; Romans 12.4 ff.
9. Another sphere in which this kind of confusion is apparent is that of work and leisure. This but reflects the more general inability of Christian theology to avoid confusion in any question involving being and doing.
10. In the widest sense, not necessarily the sacrament as such.
11. St John of the Cross, *Dark Night*, bk. II, ch. III. My emphasis.
12. Cf. Ephesians 6.10 ff.
13. St Teresa of Avila, *The Interior Castle*: Seventh Mansion, ch. IV.
14. 'No one who does not follow the path of union with God can be a theologian.' Vladimir Lossky, *The Mystical Theology of the Eastern Church*, p. 39.
15. *De Oratione* 60, under Nilus.
16. St Irenaeus, *Adversus Haereses*, IV.20.7.

## CHAPTER 9

1. See above, pp. 126–7.
2. It may be noted that any kind of innocent suffering has a potential of vicariousness. The fact of being hurt by others can be taken up in terms of vicariousness; so can the plain fact of being hurt.
3. Genesis 1.28.
4. Romans 8.21.
5. For the development of this idea, see the writings of the contemporary Romanian Orthodox theologian, Fr. Dumitru Staniloae.
6. Archimandrite Sophrony.
7. Sister Benedicta Ward, S.L.G., *The Wisdom of the Desert Fathers*, Introduction, p. xiii.
8. Archimandrite Sophrony.
9. For a detailed study, see John Saward, 'The Fool for Christ's Sake in Monasticism', in A. M. Allchin, ed., *Theology and Prayer*.
10. 1 Corinthians 1.21.
11. Rule of the Community of the Sisters of the Love of God.
12. Gilbert Shaw, *The Christian Solitary*, p. 7.
13. St John 5.24.
14. For the idea of progression or *epektasis*, see St Gregory of Nyssa, *passim*.
15. Julian of Norwich, *Revelations of Divine Love*, ch. 14.

# Bibliography: General

*The place of publication is London, except where otherwise indicated.*

Adkins, Arthur W. H., *Merit and Responsibility* (A study in Greek values). Oxford, Clarendon Press, 1960.
Anson, H., and others, *Concerning Prayer*. Macmillan 1923. Ch. 1, 'God and the world's pain', B. H. Streeter; ch. 5, 'Repentance and hope', by the author of *Pro Christo et Ecclesia*; ch. 12, 'Faith, prayer, and the world's order', pt. 2: 'Divine omnipotence and moral freedom', A. C. Turner; ch. 13, 'The Devil', R. G. Collingwood.
Berdyaev, N., *The Russian Revolution* (Two essays on its implications in religion and psychology). Sheed & Ward 1931. First essay: 'Russian religious psychology and communistic atheism'.
Bergstrom, L., *The Alternatives and Consequences of Actions* (An essay on certain fundamental notions in teleological ethics). Stockholm Studies in Philosophy, 4. Stockholm, Almqvist & Wiksell, 1966.
Boyce Gibson, A., *The Religion of Dostoevsky*. SCM Press 1973.
Buber, M., *I and Thou*. Edinburgh, T. & T. Clark, 1959.
Camus, Albert, *The Plague*. Hamish Hamilton 1948.
——, *The Rebel*. Hamish Hamilton 1960.
Casey, John, ed., *Morality and Moral Reasoning* (Five essays in ethics). Methuen 1971. Essay 5: 'Actions and consequences', John Casey.
Cruickshank, John, *Albert Camus and the Literature of Revolt*. Oxford University Press 1970.
Dawe, Donald G., *The Form of a Servant* (An historical analysis of the kenotic motif). Philadelphia, The Westminster Press, 1963.
Dominian, Jack, *Cycles of Affirmation* (Psychological essays in Christian living). Darton, Longman & Todd 1975.
Dostoevsky, Fyodor, *The Brothers Karamazov*, 2 vols. Tr., with an introduction, by David Magarshack. Penguin Books 1958.

Du Bose, W. P., *The Gospel in the Gospels*. Longmans, Green 1906.
——, *The Gospel according to St Paul*. Longmans, Green 1907.
——, *Turning Points in My Life*. Longmans, Green 1912.
Dyson, A. E., *Freedom in Love*. SPCK 1975.
Fuchs, J., *Natural Law*. Dublin, Gill & Son, 1965.
Gorodetzky, N., *The Humiliated Christ in Modern Russian Thought*. SPCK 1938.
Hadfield, Alice Mary, *An Introduction to Charles Williams*. Robert Hale 1959.
Jones, J. Walter, *Historical Introduction to the Theory of Law*. Oxford, Clarendon Press, 1940.
Kolnai, Aurel, 'Forgiveness'. A paper, read in 1973.
Lake, Frank, *Clinical Theology*. Darton, Longman & Todd 1966.
Lloyd-Jones, Hugh, *The Justice of Zeus*, Sather Classical Lectures, vol. 41. Berkeley, University of California Press, 1971.
McIntyre, John, *Prophet of Penitence* (A lecture delivered in Rhu Church on Thursday, 24 February 1972 to commemorate the centenary of the death of the Revd John McLeod Campbell, D.D., minister of the parish 1825–31). Edinburgh, The Saint Andrew Press, 1972.
Mackintosh, H. R., *The Christian Experience of Forgiveness*. Nisbet 1927.
McLeod Campbell, J., *Reminiscences and Reflections*, ed. D. Campbell. Macmillan 1873.
Moberly, R. C., *Christ Our Life*. John Murray 1902.
——, *Problems and Principles*. John Murray 1904.
Moberly, W. H., 'The Theology of Dr Du Bose', *JTS*, January 1908.
——, 'Robert Campbell Moberly', *JTS*, October 1904.
——, 'Moral Indignation'. A paper, undated (but after 1922).
——, *Responsibility*. Riddell Memorial Lectures, Durham, 21st ser. Oxford University Press 1951.
Mooney, Christopher F., *Teilhard de Chardin and the Mystery of Christ*. Collins 1966.
Mortimer, R. C., *Origins of Private Penance*. Oxford, Clarendon Press, 1939.
Oman, John, *Grace and Personality*. Collins, Fontana 1960.

Pelz, Werner and Lotte, *God is No More*, ch. 8: 'Forgiveness', and the postscripts to ch. 8. Pelican Books 1968.
Rust, Eric C., *Evolutionary Philosophies and Contemporary Theology*. Philadelphia, The Westminster Press, 1969.
Schmemann, A., *The World as Sacrament*. Darton, Longman & Todd 1974.
Shideler, Mary McDermott, *The Theology of Romantic Love* (A study in the writings of Charles Williams). New York, Harper, 1962.
Stone, Julius, *Human Law and Human Justice*. Sydney, Maitland Publications, 1965.
——, *The Province and Function of Law*. Stevens 1961.
Taylor, Vincent, *Forgiveness and Reconciliation*. Macmillan 1941.
Teilhard de Chardin, P., *Le Milieu Divin*. Collins, Fontana 1970.
——, *Human Energy*. Collins 1969.
——, *The Phenomenon of Man*. Collins 1960.
——, *Activation of Energy*. Collins 1970.
——, *The Future of Man*. Collins 1964.
——, *Man's Place in Nature*. Collins 1966.
Telfer, W., *The Forgiveness of Sins* (An essay in the history of Christian doctrine and practice). SCM Press 1959.
Temple, William, *The Nature of Personality*. Macmillan 1911.
Tournier, Paul, *Guilt and Grace*. Hodder & Stoughton 1962.
Urang, Gunnar, *Shadows of Heaven* (A study of J. R. R. Tolkien, C. S. Lewis, and Charles Williams). SCM Press 1971.
Watkins, Oscar D., *A History of Penance*, 2 vols. Longmans, Green 1920.
Webb, C. C. J., *Studies in the History of Natural Theology*. Oxford, Clarendon Press, 1970.
Williams, Charles, *He Came Down from Heaven* (and *The Forgiveness of Sins*). Faber & Faber 1950.
——, *The Image of the City and Other Essays*, with an introduction by Anne Ridler. Oxford University Press 1958.
——, *Descent into Hell*. Faber & Faber 1937.
——, *All Hallows Eve*. Faber & Faber 1945.
Williams, Daniel Day, *The Spirit and Forms of Love*. Nisbet 1968.
Williams, Watkin W., *The Moral Theology of the Sacrament of Penance*. Mowbray 1917.
Zernov, N., *Three Russian Prophets* (Khomiakov, Dostoevsky, Soloviev). SCM Press 1944.

# Bibliography: Thematic

## THE ATONEMENT

Abelard, Peter, *Commentaria in Epistolam Pauli ad Romanos*, in *Petri Abaelardi Opera Theologica*, vol. 1. Turnhout, Brepols, 1969.
——, *Epitome Theologiae Christianae*, esp. ch. 23: 'Cur Deus Homo?' *PL* 178, cols. 1685–1758.
——, *Ethics (Scito te ipsum)*. *PL* 178, cols. 633–78. Also the edn. of D. E. Luscombe. Oxford, Clarendon Press, 1971.
——, *Letters*. *PL* 178, cols. 113–378. Also the English edn. of C. K. Scott Moncrieff. Chapman 1925.
Aulén, Gustaf, *Christus Victor*. SPCK 1970.
Baird, J. Arthur, *The Justice of God in the Teaching of Jesus*. SCM Press 1963.
Barry, F. R., *The Atonement*. Hodder & Stoughton 1968.
Bernard, St, *Capitula Haeresum Petri Abaelardi*. *PL* 182, cols. 1049–54.
——, *Tractatus de erroribus Petri Abaelardi*. *PL* 182, cols. 1053–72. (Letter 190, to Pope Innocent II).
——, *Letters*. *PL* 182, nos. 187–9, 192, 193, 327, 330–36, 338. Also, 194 (Pope Innocent, against the heresies of Peter Abelard); 326 (William of St Thierry to the Abbot of Clairvaux and the Bishop of Chartres); 337 (The bishops of France to Pope Innocent).
Brierley, H. E., and others, *What the Cross Means to Me*. Clarke 1943.
Dale, R. W., *The Atonement* (The Congregational Union Lecture for 1875). Hodder & Stoughton 1875.
Dillistone, F. W., *The Christian Understanding of Atonement*. Nisbet 1968.
Dinsmore, Charles Allen, *Atonement in Literature and Life*. Constable 1906.
Du Bose, W. P., *The Soteriology of the New Testament*. Longmans, Green 1907.

——, *High Priesthood and Sacrifice*. Longmans, Green 1908.
Godet, Frédéric, and others, *The Atonement in Modern Religious Thought*. Clarke 1902.
Gore, Charles, *Belief in Christ*. Ch. x, on the atonement. John Murray 1922.
Grensted, L. W., *A Short History of the Doctrine of the Atonement*. Manchester University Press and Longmans, Green 1920.
Irenaeus, St, *Adversus Haereses PG* 7. Also the English edn. of John Keble. Oxford, London, and Cambridge, Parker and Rivingtons, 1872.
Johnson, Ernest W., *Suffering, Punishment and Atonement*. Macmillan 1919.
Kirk, Kenneth E., 'The Atonement', essay no. 8 in *Essays Catholic and Critical*, ed. E. G. Selwyn. SPCK 1926.
Lawson, John, *The Biblical Theology of St Irenaeus*. Epworth Press 1948.
Lloyd, Roger B., *The Stricken Lute* (An account of the life of Peter Abelard). Lovat Dickson 1932.
Lofthouse, W. F., *Ethics and Atonement*. Methuen 1906.
Lyttelton, Arthur, 'The Atonement', s. 7 of *Lux Mundi*, ed. Charles Gore, John Murray 1890.
Mackintosh, H. R., *Some Aspects of Christian Belief*. Hodder & Stoughton 1923.
Mackintosh, R., *Historic Theories of Atonement*. Hodder & Stoughton 1920.
McLeod Campbell, J., *The Nature of the Atonement*. Macmillan 1867.
Maldwyn Hughes, H., *What is the Atonement?* Clarke (undated).
Maurice, F. D., *The Doctrine of Sacrifice*. Macmillan 1893.
Meyendorff, J., *Christ in Eastern Christian Thought*. Washington and Cleveland, Corpus Books, 1969.
——, *Byzantine Theology*. Oxford, Mowbray, 1975.
Micklem, Nathaniel, *The Doctrine of Our Redemption*. Eyre & Spottiswoode 1943.
Moberly, R. C., *Atonement and Personality*. John Murray 1932.
——, *Sorrow, Sin and Beauty*. Rivingtons 1889.
Moberly, W. H., 'The Meaning of Atonement'. A paper read to the Synthetic Society, 29 April 1909.
Moltmann, Jurgen, *The Crucified God*. SCM Press 1974.
Morris, Leon, *Glory in the Cross*. Hodder & Stoughton 1966.

Moule, C. F. D., *The Sacrifice of Christ*. Hodder & Stoughton 1956.
Mozley, J. K., *The Doctrine of the Atonement*. Duckworth 1915.
Murray, A. Victor, *Abelard and St Bernard*, Manchester and New York, Manchester University Press and Barnes & Noble, 1967.
Oxenham, H. N., *The Catholic Doctrine of the Atonement*. W. H. Allen 1895.
Paul, Robert S., *The Atonement and the Sacraments*. Hodder & Stoughton 1961.
Quick, O. C., *Doctrines of the Creed*, pt. III: 'The Christian doctrine of salvation'. Nisbet 1938.
Rashdall, Hastings, 'Dr Moberly's Theory of the Atonement', in *JTS*, January 1902.
——, *The Idea of Atonement in Christian Theology* (Bampton Lectures 1915). Macmillan 1919.
Richard, Louis, *The Mystery of the Redemption*. Baltimore, Helicon, 1965.
Rupp, Gordon, 'Moberly's *Atonement and Personality*', in *The Expository Times*, January 1953.
Sanday, William, ed., *Different Conceptions of Priesthood and Sacrifice* (A report of a conference held at Oxford, 1899). Longmans, Green 1900.
——, *The Life of Christ in Recent Research*. Oxford, Clarendon Press, 1907.
Scott Lidgett, John, *The Spiritual Principle of the Atonement*. Kelly 1897.
Sikes, J. G., *Peter Abailard*. Cambridge University Press 1932.
Smith, David, *The Atonement in the Light of History and the Modern Spirit*. Hodder & Stoughton 1918.
Soderblom, Nathan, *The Mystery of the Cross*. SCM Press 1933.
Solle, Dorothee, *Christ the Representative*. SCM Press 1967.
Taylor, Vincent, *The Atonement in New Testament Teaching*. Epworth Press 1963.
——, *The Cross of Christ*. Macmillan 1956.
Tennant, F. R., *The Concept of Sin*. Cambridge, Cambridge University Press, 1912.
Trethowan, Illtyd, *The Absolute and the Atonement*. Allen & Unwin 1971.
Turner, H. E. W., *The Patristic Doctrine of Redemption*. Mowbray 1952.

Ward, Sister Benedicta, ed., *The Influence of Saint Bernard*. Oxford, SLG Press, 1976.
Weingart, Richard E., *The Logic of Divine Love* (A critical analysis of the soteriology of Peter Abailard). Oxford, Clarendon Press, 1970.
Whale, J. S., *Victor and Victim*. Cambridge, Cambridge University Press, 1960.
Williams, Watkin, *Saint Bernard of Clairvaux*, ch. XIII: 'The Theology of the Schools'. Manchester, Manchester University Press, 1953.
Wilson, J. M., *How Christ Saves Us* or *The Gospel of Atonement* (Hulsean Lectures 1898–9). Macmillan 1905.

## COMPARATIVE RELIGION

Appleton, George, *On the Eightfold Path* (Christian presence amid Buddhism). SCM Press 1961.
Bowker, John, *Problems of Suffering in Religions of the World*. Cambridge, Cambridge University Press, 1970.
Conze, Edward, *Thirty Years of Buddhist Studies*. Oxford, Bruno Cassirer, 1967.
——, ed., *Buddhist Scriptures*. Penguin Books 1973.
Coomaraswamy, Ananda K., *Buddha and the Gospel of Buddhism*. New York, Harper Torchbooks, 1964.
Dalai Lama, *My Land and my People*, Appendix I: 'The Religion of Tibet'. Weidenfeld & Nicolson 1962.
Eliade, Mircea, *Yoga—Immortality and Freedom*. Routledge & Kegan Paul 1958.
Humphreys, Christmas, *Buddhism*. Penguin Books 1951.
——, ed., *The Wisdom of Buddhism*. Michael Joseph 1960.
Johnston, William, *The Still Point* (Reflections on Zen and Christian Mysticism). New York, Fordham University Press, 1970.
Koyama, Kosuke, *Waterbuffalo Theology*. SCM Press 1974.
Ling, Trevor, *Buddha, Marx, and God*. Macmillan 1966.
Olcott, Henry S., *A Buddhist Catechism* (according to the Sinhalese canon). Madras, Henry S. Olcott, 1886.
Panikkar, Raymond, *The Unknown Christ of Hinduism*. Darton, Longman & Todd 1968.
Parrinder, Geoffrey, *Worship in the World's Religions*. Sheldon Press 1961.

———, *Mysticism in the World's Religions.* Sheldon Press 1976.
———, *Avatar and Incarnation.* Faber & Faber 1970.
Radhakrishnan, S., ed., *The Bhagavadgita.* Allen & Unwin 1948.
Raju, P. T., *The Philosophical Traditions of India.* Allen & Unwin 1971.
Rhys Davids, T. W., *Buddhism.* SPCK (undated).
Singh, Sant Kirpal Singh Ji., 'Man, Know Thyself'. A talk, 1954.
Smart, Ninian, *The Religious Experience of Mankind.* Collins, Fontana 1971.
Spiro, Melford, E., *Buddhism and Society.* Allen & Unwin 1971.
Thomas, Edward J., *The Life of Buddha* (as legend and history). Kegan Paul, Trench & Trubner 1931.
———, *The History of Buddhist Thought.* Kegan Paul, Trench & Trubner 1933.
Zaehner, R. C., *Hinduism.* Oxford University Press 1972.
———, *At Sundry Times* (An essay in the comparison of religions). Faber & Faber 1958.
———, ed., *Hindu Scriptures.* Dent 1972.

## CRIMINOLOGY—THE THEORY OF PUNISHMENT

Acton, H. B., ed., *The Philosophy of Punishment.* Macmillan 1969.
Andenaes, Johannes, 'The General Preventive Effects of Punishment', in *University of Pennsylvania Law Review*, vol. 114, no. 7, May 1966.
Anon, *The Ethics of Punishment.* Madras, Methodist Publishing House (undated).
Bentham, Jeremy, *Theory of Legislation.* Kegan Paul, Trench & Trubner 1908.
———, 'Principles of Penal Law', in vol. 1 of *The Works of Jeremy Bentham*, ed. John Bowring. Edinburgh, William Tait, 1843.
———, *An Introduction to the Principles of Morals and Legislation*, ed. J. H. Burns and H. L. A. Hart. University of London, Athlone Press 1970.
Bosanquet, Bernard, *The Philosophical Theory of the State.* Macmillan 1910.
———, *Some Suggestions in Ethics.* Macmillan 1918.
Bradley, F. H., *Ethical Studies*, essay I: 'The Vulgar Notion of Responsibility in Connection with the Theories of Free-will and Responsibility'. Oxford, Clarendon Press, 1927.

## BIBLIOGRAPHY: THEMATIC

De Pauley, W. C., *Punishment, Human and Divine*. SPCK 1925.
Emmet, Dorothy, 'Justice', in *Aristotelian Society*, supplementary volume XLIII. 1969.
Ewing, A. C., *The Morality of Punishment*. Kegan Paul, Trench & Trubner 1929.
Ezorsky, Gertrude, ed., *Philosophical Perspectives on Punishment*. Albany, State University of New York Press, 1972.
Gerber, Rudolph J., and McAnany, Patrick D., eds., *Contemporary Punishment*. Notre Dame, Indiana: University of Notre Dame Press, 1972.
Grupp, Stanley E., ed., *Theories of Punishment*. Bloomington, Indiana University Press, 1971.
Hart, H. L. A., *The Morality of the Criminal Law*. Oxford University Press 1965.
——, *Law, Liberty and Morality*. Oxford University Press 1966.
——, *Punishment and Responsibility*. Oxford, Clarendon Press, 1968.
Hegel, G., *Philosophy of Right*, tr., with notes, by T. M. Knox. Oxford, Clarendon Press, 1942.
Honderich, Ted, *Punishment* (The supposed justifications). Penguin Books 1971.
Kant, I., *Lectures on Ethics*, tr. L. Infield, with an introduction by J. Macmurray. Methuen 1930.
——, *The Philosophy of Law*, tr. W. Hastie. Edinburgh, T. & T. Clark, 1887.
Kenny, C. S., *Outlines of Criminal Law*. Cambridge, Cambridge University Press, 1926.
Longford, Lord (Pakenham, Lord), *The Idea of Punishment*. Chapman 1961.
——, *Causes of Crime*. Weidenfeld & Nicolson 1958.
McTaggart, J. M. E., *Studies in Hegelian Cosmology*. Cambridge, Cambridge University Press, 1901.
Mercier, Charles, *Crime and Criminals*. University of London Press 1918.
Mill, John Stuart, 'Utilitarianism', in J. Plamenatz, *The English Utilitarians*. Oxford, Blackwell, 1949.
——, *An Examination of Sir William Hamilton's Philosophy*, ch. XXVI: 'On the Freedom of the Will'. Longmans, Green 1865.
Moberly, Sir Walter (W. H. Moberly), *The Ethics of Punishment*. Faber & Faber 1968.

——, 'Some Ambiguities in the Retributive Theory of Punishment'. A paper read to the Aristotelian Society, 1925.
Moule, C. F. D., 'Punishment and Retribution' (An attempt to delimit their scope in NT thought). Sartryck ur *Svensk Exegetisk Arsbok* xxx, 1965.
Oppenheimer, Heinrich, *The Rationale of Punishment*. University of London Press 1913.
Pailthorpe, Grace W., *Studies in the Psychology of Delinquency*. HMSO 1932.
Phillipson, Coleman, *Three Criminal Law Reformers* (Beccaria, Bentham, Romilly). Dent 1923.
Pieper, Josef, *Justice*. Faber & Faber 1957.
Plamenatz, John, *The English Utilitarians*. Oxford, Blackwell, 1949.
Rashdall, Hastings, *The Theory of Good and Evil*, vol. I. Oxford University Press 1924.
Selby-Bigge, L. A., ed., *British Moralists*, vol. I. Oxford, Clarendon Press, 1897.
Strauss, E. B., 'Moral Responsibility and the Law'. President's address, Royal Society of Medicine. *Proceedings*, vol. 47, no. 1, January 1954.
Thomas, D. A., 'Theories of Punishment in the Court of Criminal Appeal', in *The Modern Law Review*, vol. 27, September 1964.
Wootton, Barbara, *Crime and the Criminal Law*. The Hamlyn Lectures, 15th ser. Stevens 1963.

## ESCHATOLOGY

Aldwinckle, Russell, *Death in the Secular City* (A study of the notion of life after death in contemporary theology and philosophy). Allen & Unwin 1972.
Catherine of Genoa, St, 'Treatise on Purgatory', in vol. XIII of The Library of Christian Classics: *Late Medieval Mysticism*, ed. Ray C. Petry. SCM Press 1957.
Dante, Alighieri, *The Divine Comedy*, 3 vols. Dent 1900.
Dodd, C. H., *The Parables of the Kingdom*. Nisbet 1935.
Farrar, Frederic W., *Eternal Hope*. Macmillan 1879.
Gayford, S. C., *The Future State*. Rivingtons 1903.
Guy, H. A., *The New Testament Doctrine of the 'Last Things'*. Oxford University Press 1948.

Hick, John, *Death and Eternal Life*. Collins 1976.
Kummel, W. G., *Promise and Fulfilment* (The Eschatological Message of Jesus). SCM Press 1969.
Lewis, C. S., *The Great Divorce*. Geoffrey Bles, The Centenary Press 1945.
Lucock, H. M., *The Intermediate State*. Longmans, Green 1904.
Newman, Cardinal, *The Dream of Gerontius*. Bagster 1971.
Paternoster, Michael, *Thou Art There Also* (God, death, and hell). SPCK 1967.
Pusey, E. B., *What is of Faith as to Everlasting Punishment?* For the Devonport Society 1880. Parker and Rivingtons 1881.
Robinson, John A. T., *Jesus and His Coming*. SCM Press 1957.
Rowell, Geoffrey, *Hell and the Victorians*. Oxford, Clarendon Press, 1974.
St Austin, Mother Mary, *The Divine Crucible* (Purgatory). Burns & Oates 1948.
Strawson, William, *Jesus and the Future Life*. Epworth Press 1970.
Wright, C. H. H., *The Intermediate State*. Nisbet 1900.

## PRAYER—SPIRITUALITY

Allchin, A. M., ed., *Theology and Prayer*. Studies Supplementary to Sobornost, no. 3. Fellowship of St Alban and St Sergius 1975.
Allison Peers, E., *Mother of Carmel* (A portrait of St Teresa of Avila). SCM Press 1961.
——, *Spirit of Flame* (A study of St John of the Cross). SCM Press 1943.
——, *Studies of the Spanish Mystics*, vol. 1. SPCK 1951.
Anon, *The Cloud of Unknowing*, tr. into modern English by Clifton Wolters. Penguin Classics 1965.
Anselm, St, *The Prayers and Meditations of St Anselm*, tr. Sister Benedicta Ward, S.L.G. Penguin Classics 1973.
Anthony, Metropolitan. *Living Prayer*. Darton, Longman & Todd 1968.
——, *School for Prayer*, Darton, Longman & Todd 1970.
——, *God and Man*. Darton, Longman & Todd 1971.
——, *Meditations on a Theme*. Mowbray 1972.
—— (with Georges LeFebvre), *Courage to Pray*. Darton, Longman & Todd 1973.

Baker, Augustine, *Holy Wisdom*. Burns & Oates 1964.
Benedict, St, *Rule for Monasteries*, tr. Leonard J. Doyle. Collegeville, Minnesota: The Liturgical Press, St John's Abbey, 1948.
Bouyer, Louis, *Introduction to Spirituality*. Darton, Longman & Todd, 1963.
Butler, Dom Cuthbert, *Western Mysticism*. 2nd edn., with afterthoughts. Constable 1951.
Carter, T. T., *Spiritual Guidance*. Rivingtons 1873.
Chapman, Dom John, *Spiritual Letters*, ed. Dom Roger Hudleston. Sheed & Ward 1935.
Chavchavadze, Marina, ed., *Man's Concern with Holiness*. The Catholic Book Club 1972.
De Besse, Ludovic, *Light on Mount Carmel* (A guide to the works of St John of the Cross). Burns Oates & Washbourne 1926.
De Caussade, J. P., *Self-abandonment to Divine Providence*, tr. Algar Thorold. Burns & Oates 1962.
Doherty, Catharine de Hueck, *Poustinia* (Christian spirituality of the East for western man). Notre Dame, Indiana: Ave Maria Press, 1975.
Fedotov, G. P., ed., *A Treasury of Russian Spirituality*. Sheed & Ward 1952.
Grou, John Nicholas, *Spiritual Maxims*. Burns & Oates 1961.
Hilton, Walter, *The Ladder of Perfection*, tr. Leo Sherley-Price. Penguin Classics 1957.
John Climacus, St, *The Ladder of Divine Ascent*, tr. Archimandrite Lazarus Moore, with an introduction by M. Heppell. Willits, California: Eastern Orthodox Books (undated).
John of the Cross, St, *Complete Works*, tr. and ed. E. Allison Peers. Wheathampstead, Anthony Clarke, 1974.
Johnston, William, *The Mysticism of the Cloud of Unknowing*. New York, Desclee, 1967.
Julian of Norwich, *Revelations of Divine Love*. Penguin Classics 1974.
Kadloubovsky, E., and Palmer, G. E. H., tr., *Early Fathers from the Philokalia*. Faber & Faber 1973.
——, *Writings from the Philokalia on the Prayer of the Heart*. Faber & Faber 1971.
——, *The Art of Prayer*, compiled by Igumen Chariton of Valamo, ed., with an introduction, by T. Ware. Faber & Faber 1966.

Knowles, David, *The English Mystical Tradition*. Burns & Oates 1961.
Lossky, Vladimir, *The Mystical Theology of the Eastern Church*. Clarke 1968.
——, *The Vision of God*. Leighton Buzzard, The Faith Press, 1973.
——, *In the Image and Likeness of God*. New York, St Vladimir's Seminary Press, 1974.
Macarius, Starets of Optino, *Russian Letters of Direction, 1834–1860*. New York, St Vladimir's Seminary Press, 1975.
Mary Clare, Mother, *Learning to Pray*. Oxford, SLG Press, 1970.
——, *Christian Maturity through Prayer*. Oxford, SLG Press, 1970.
——, *The Apostolate of Prayer*. Oxford, SLG Press, 1972.
——, *Silence and Prayer*. Oxford, SLG Press (undated).
——, *Prayer: Encountering the Depths*. Oxford, SLG Press, 1973.
——, *Carmelite Ascent*. Oxford, SLG Press, 1973.
Merton, Thomas, *Contemplative Prayer*. Darton, Longman & Todd 1973.
Molinari, Paul, *Julian of Norwich*. The Catholic Book Club 1959.
Monk of the Eastern Church, *Orthodox Spirituality*. SPCK 1974.
O'Mahony, Christopher, ed., *St Thérèse of Lisieux* (by those who knew her). Dublin, Veritas Publications, 1975.
Poulain, A., *The Graces of Interior Prayer*. Kegan Paul, Trench & Trubner 1928.
Saudreau, A., *The Life of Union with God*. Burns Oates & Washbourne 1927.
——, *The Mystical State, its Nature and Phases*. Burns Oates & Washbourne 1924.
——, *The Degrees of the Spiritual Life*, vol. II. R. and T. Washbourne 1907.
Shaw, Gilbert, *A Pilgrim's Book of Prayers*. Mowbray 1955.
——, *The Face of Love*. Oxford, SLG Press, 1977.
Sophrony, Archimandrite, *The Undistorted Image*. Faith Press 1958.
Stein, Edith, *The Science of the Cross* (A study of St John of the Cross). Burns & Oates 1960.
Steuart, R. H. J., *The Mystical Doctrine of St John of the Cross* (An abridgement, with introduction). Sheed & Ward 1953.

Tanquerey, A., *The Spiritual Life*. New York, Desclee, 1930.
Tauler, John, *The Following of Christ*. Burns, Oates & Washbourne 1886.
Teresa of Avila, St, *The Interior Castle*. Sands 1945.
——, *Life*. Penguin Classics 1957.
——, *Way of Perfection*. Burns & Oates 1961.
Thibaut, Dom Raymond, *Union with God According to the Letters of Direction of Dom Marmion*. Sands 1960.
Thomas, Father, and Gabriel, Father, *Saint Teresa of Avila*. Dublin, Clonmore & Reynolds 1963.
Trueman Dicken, E. W., *The Crucible of Love* (A study of the mysticism of St Teresa of Avila and St John of the Cross). Darton, Longman & Todd 1963.
Underhill, Evelyn, *The Letters of Evelyn Underhill*, ed. Charles Williams. Longmans, Green 1943.
Ware, Archimandrite Kallistos, *The Power of the Name* (The Jesus Prayer in Orthodox Spirituality). Oxford, SLG Press, 1974.

# SOLITARIES

Allchin, A. M., ed., *Communion and Solitude*. Oxford, SLG Press, 1977.
Anon, *The Ancrene Riwle*, tr. into modern English by M. B. Salu. Burns & Oates 1967.
Anson, Peter, *The Call of the Desert*. SPCK 1964.
Chitty, Derwas, *The Desert, a City*. Oxford, Blackwell, 1966.
Curtis, Geoffrey, *William of Glasshampton: Friar, Monk, Solitary*. SPCK 1947.
Damian, St Peter, 'The Book of "The Lord be with you" ', In *St Peter Damian* (selected writings), ed. Patricia McNulty. Faber & Faber 1959.
Desert Fathers, *The Sayings of the Desert Fathers* (The Alphabetical Collection), tr. Sister Benedicta Ward, S.L.G. London and Michigan, Mowbray and Cistercian Publications, 1975.
——, *The Wisdom of the Desert Fathers* (The Anonymous Series), tr., with an introduction, Sister Benedicta Ward, S.L.G. Oxford, SLG Press, 1975.
Lacarrière, Jacques, *The God-Possessed*. Allen & Unwin 1963.
Leclercq, Dom Jean, *Alone with God*. The Catholic Book Club 1962.

Merton, Thomas, *The Power and Meaning of Love*. Sheldon Press 1976.
——, *The Silent Life*, esp. s. III: 'The Hermit Life'. Sheldon Press 1975.
——, *Contemplation in a World of Action*, pt. 2: 'The Case for Eremitism'. Allen & Unwin 1971.
Rolle, Richard, *The Fire of Love*, tr. into modern English by Clifton Wolters. Penguin Books 1972.
Shaw, Gilbert, *The Christian Solitary*. Oxford, SLG Press, 1971.

## THEODICY—SUFFERING—EVIL

Ahern, M. B., *The Problem of Evil*. Routledge & Kegan Paul 1971.
Autton, Norman, ed., *From Fear to Faith* (Studies of suffering and wholeness'. SPCK 1971.
Boros, Ladislaus, *Pain and Providence*. Burns & Oates 1966.
De Beausobre, Iulia, *Creative Suffering*. Dacre Press 1954.
Driver, S. R., ed., *The Book of Job*. Oxford, Clarendon Press, 1906.
Ellul, Jacques, *Violence*. SCM Press 1970.
Farrer, Austin, *Love Almighty and Ills Unlimited* (An essay on providence and evil, containing the Nathaniel Taylor Lectures for 1961). Collins 1962.
France, Malcolm, *The Paradox of Guilt*. Hodder & Stoughton 1967.
Hibbert, Christopher, *The Roots of Evil*. Weidenfeld & Nicolson 1963.
Hick, John, *Evil and the God of Love*. Collins, Fontana 1968.
——, *God and the Universe of Faiths*, ch. 4: 'God, evil, and mystery'; ch. 5: 'The problem of evil in the first and last things'. Macmillan 1973.
Houselander, F. Caryll, *Guilt*. Sheed & Ward 1952.
James, John, *Why Evil?* Pelican Books 1960.
Jung, C. G., *Answer to Job*. Routledge & Kegan Paul 1954.
Kitamori, Kazoh, *Theology of the Pain of God*. SCM Press 1966.
Kraeling, Emil G., *The Book of the Ways of God* (Job). SPCK 1938.
Lewis, C. S., *The Problem of Pain*. The Centenary Press, 1940.
Mackie, J. L., 'Evil and Omnipotence', ch. 5 of *The Philosophy of Religion*, ed. B. Mitchell. Oxford University Press 1971.

Neil-Smith, Christopher, *The Exorcist and the Possessed*. St Ives, James Pike, 1974.
Pope, Marvin H., *Job* (The Anchor Bible). New York, Doubleday, 1965.
Rankin, O. S., *Israel's Wisdom Literature*. Edinburgh, T. & T. Clark, 1936.
Richards, John, *But Deliver Us from Evil*. Darton, Longman & Todd 1974.
Ricoeur, Paul, *The Symbolism of Evil*. Boston, The Beacon Press, 1967.
Rowley, H. H., ed., *Job* (The Century Bible). Nelson 1970.
Schoonenberg, Piet, *Man and Sin*. Sheed & Ward 1965.
Simon, Ulrich E., *A Theology of Auschwitz*. Gollancz 1967.
Snaith, Norman H., *The Book of Job*. SCM Press 1968.
Staniloae, Dumitru, 'The Cross on the Gift of the World', in *Sobornost*, ser. 6, no. 2, Winter 1971.
——, *The Victory of the Cross*. Oxford, SLG Press (undated).
Walker, John, *Disasters*. Studio Vista 1973.
Wenham, J. W., *The Goodness of God*. Inter-Varsity Press 1974.
White, Douglas, *Forgiveness and Suffering*, Cambridge, Cambridge University Press, 1913.

# Index of Names

Abelard, Peter 22–9
Acton, H. B. 84
Adam 52
Allen, Francis A. 94
Ancel, Marc 100
Augustine, St 13–14, 52
Aulén, Gustaf 24

Beccaria 90
Benedicta (Ward), Sister 144
Benn, Stanley I. 95, 98
Bentham, Jeremy 90–91, 93, 97–8
Bernard, St 29
Bosanquet, Bernard 85, 86, 100
Bradley, F. H. 83, 85, 87

Camus, Albert 10
Cappadocian Fathers 4
Catherine of Genoa, St 118
Coomaraswamy, Ananda 37

Dalai Lama 37
Dostoevsky, Fyodor 10
Dreyfus, Alfred 67, 80

Evagrius (Ponticus) 4, 134
Ezekiel 51

Garafalo 94
Genesis 3, 142
Glueck, Sheldon 96
Gregory of Sinai, St 124
Grensted, L. W. 23, 27

Hegel, Georg 83, 85–7
Honderich, Ted 84, 89
Humphreys, Christmas 37, 38, 39

Irenaeus, St 13–14, 16–22, 23, 28, 135
Israel 126

Job 39–48
John, St 19, 26, 148
John of the Cross, St 110, 130
Julian of Norwich 148

Kant, Immanuel 82, 83

Luke, St 6

McTaggart, J. M. E. 83, 84, 87, 95
Mary Clare, Mother 125
Matthew, St 53
Mill, J. S. 92
Moberly, R. C. 118–21, 153–5
Moberly, Sir Walter 61–81, 82, 83, 84, 85, 101, 102, 105, 117, 153

Olcott, H. S. 51
Oresteia 51

Packer, Herbert L. 89
Paul, St 4, 17, 18, 21, 27, 52, 127, 128, 142, 145
Peters, Richard S. 95, 98
Plamenatz, John 94

Quinton, Anthony M. 93

Rashdall, Hastings 98–9

Shaw, Gilbert 147
Sikes, J. G. 26
Silving, Helen 95, 100
Sophrony, Archimandrite 143, 145
Spinoza 62

Teilhard de Chardin, Pierre 4, 5, 14
Teresa of Avila, St 132
Theophan the Recluse 125

Williams, Charles 4